D1236246

Collected Poems

By F. T. Prince

F. T. Prince

Collected Poems

The Sheep Meadow Press
New York City
1979

Published in 1979
by The Sheep Meadow Press
145 Central Park West
New York, NY 10023

ISBN 0 8180 1547 0 [cloth]
      0 8180 1548 9 [paper]
Library of Congress Catalog No 78–56100

Printed and bound in Great Britain at
The Camelot Press Ltd, Southampton

Contents

Prefatory Note

This book brings together the contents of *The Doors of Stone* (Rupert Hart-Davis, 1963) and three later publications: *Memoirs in Oxford* (Fulcrum Press, 1970), *Drypoints of the Hasidim* (Menard Press, 1975) and *Afterword on Rupert Brooke* (Menard Press, 1977). *The Doors of Stone* included all the poems I wanted to reprint from *Poems* (Faber & Faber, 1938) and *Soldiers Bathing* (Fortune Press, 1954). These are retained in the present collection. Two or three short pieces written since 1963 have been added. Some of the later poems have been revised, and *Memoirs in Oxford* has also been reshaped. But I have not tried to alter the general tone and character of any of the poems, and I have resisted the temptation to suppress some which I no longer care for.

I am grateful to my successive publishers both for bringing out the original editions and for allowing the poems to reappear.

F. T. P.

Early Poems

to my parents

An Epistle to a Patron

My lord, hearing lately of your opulence in promises and your house
Busy with parasites, of your hands full of favours, your statutes
Admirable as music, and no fear of your arms not prospering, I have
Considered how to serve you and breed from my talents
These few secrets which I shall make plain
To your intelligent glory. You should understand that I have
    plotted,
Being in command of all the ordinary engines
Of defence and offence, a hundred and fifteen buildings
Less others less complete: complete, some are courts of serene stone,
Some the civil structures of a war-like elegance as bridges,
Sewers, aqueducts and citadels of brick, with which I declare the
    fact
That your nature is to vanquish. For these I have acquired a
    knowledge
Of the habits of numbers and of various tempers, and skill in setting
Firm sets of pure bare members which will rise, hanging together
Like an argument, with beams, ties and sistering pilasters:
The lintels and windows with mouldings as round as a girl's chin;
    thresholds
To libraries; halls that cannot be entered without a sensation as of
    myrrh
By your vermilion officers, your sages and dancers. There will be
    chambers
Like the recovery of a sick man, your closet waiting not
Less suitably shadowed than the heart, and the coffers of a ceiling
To reflect your diplomatic taciturnities. You may commission
Hospitals, huge granaries that will smile to bear your filial plunders,
And stables washed with a silver lime in whose middle tower seated
In the slight acridity you may watch
The copper thunder kept in the sulky flanks of your horse, a rolling
    field
Of necks glad to be groomed, the strong crupper, the edged hoof

And the long back, seductive and rebellious to saddles.
And barracks, fortresses, in need of no vest save light, light
That to me is breath, food and drink, I live by effects of light, I live
To catch it, to break it, as an orator plays off
Against each other and his theme his casual gems, and so with light,
Twisted in strings, plucked, crossed or knotted or crumbled
As it may be allowed to be by leaves,
Or clanged back by lakes and rocks or otherwise beaten,
Or else spilt and spread like a feast of honey, dripping
Through delightful voids and creeping along long fractures,
      brimming
Carved canals, bowls and lachrymatories with pearls: all this the
      work
Of now advancing, now withdrawing faces, whose use I know.
I know what slabs thus will be soaked to a thumb's depth by the sun,
And where to rob them, what colour stifles in your intact quarries,
      what
Sand silted in your river-gorges will well mix with the dust of
      flint; I know
What wood to cut by what moon in what weather
Of your sea-winds, your hill-wind: therefore tyrant, let me learn
Your high-ways, ways of sandstone, roads of the oakleaf, and
      your sea-ways.
Send me to dig dry graves, exposing what you want: I must
Attend your orgies and debates (let others apply for austerities),
      admit me
To your witty table, stuff me with urban levities, feed me, bind me
To a prudish luxury, free me thus, and with a workshop
From my household consisting
Of a pregnant wife, one female and one boy child and an elder
      bastard
With other properties; these let me regard, let me neglect, and let
What I begin be finished. Save me, noble sir, from the agony
Of starved and privy explorations such as those I stumble
From a hot bed to make, to follow lines to which the night-sky
Holds only faint contingencies. These flights with no end but failure,
And failure not to end them, these palliate or prevent.

I wish for liberty, let me then be tied: and seeing too much
I aspire to be constrained by your emblems of birth and triumph,
And between the obligations of your future and the checks of
    actual state
To flourish, adapt the stubs of an interminable descent, and place
The crested key to confident vaults; with a placid flurry of petals,
And bosom and lips, will stony functionaries support
The persuasion, so beyond proof, of your power. I will record
In peculiar scrolls your alien alliances,
Fit an apartment for your eastern hostage, extol in basalt
Your father, praise with white festoons the goddess your lady;
And for your death which will be mine prepare
An encasement as if of solid blood. And so let me
Forget, let me remember, that this is stone, stick, metal, trash
Which I will pile and hack, my hands will stain and bend
(None better knowing how to gain from the slow pains of a marble
Bruised, breathing strange climates). Being pressed as I am, being
    broken
By wealth and poverty, torn between strength and weakness, take
    me, choose
To relieve me, to receive of me, and must you not agree
As you have been to some—a great giver of banquets, of respite
    from swords,
Who shook out figured cloths, who rained coin,
A donor of laurel and of grapes, a font of profuse intoxicants—
    and so,
To be so too for me? And none too soon, since the panting mind
Rather than barren will be prostitute, and once
I served a herd of merchants; but since I will be faithful
And my virtue is such, though far from home let what is yours
    be mine, and this be a match
As many have been proved, enduring exiles and blazed
Not without issue in returning shows: your miserly freaks
Your envies, racks and poisons not out of mind
Although not told, since often borne—indeed how should it be
That you employed them less than we? but now be flattered a little
To indulge the extravagant gist of this communication,

For my pride puts all in doubt and at present I have no patience,
I have simply hope, and I submit me
To your judgement which will be just.

To a Man on his Horse

Only the Arab stallion will I
Envy you. Along the water
You dance him with the morning on his flanks.
In the frosty morning that his motions flatter
He kindles, and where the winter's in the wood,
I watch you dance him out on delicate shanks.
And lashes fall on a dark eye,
He sheds a silvery mane, he shapes
His thin nostrils like a fop's.
And to do honour to his whiteness
In remembrance of his ancient blood,
I have wished to become his groom,
And so his smouldering body comb
In a simple and indecorous sweetness.

In the Wood

The afternoon fills the grey wood
With a faint milk of mists.
As we walk some cloud suggests
A pink soft sheaf. And I would
Suddenly I were dead,
So that all were out of your mind
That love is in hope to find
And so we seek: that freed
Of all but being, you stood
With a vacant glance,
Or might in the grey air dance
With cheeks that match the cloud:
That within the cold wood
Like a vast eye at gaze,
A miraculous life that strays
Through votive solitude,
You loitered: that fever over,
To which my passion lit
Dry sticks of unlucky wit,
And the silence were your lover.

The Tears of a Muse in America

I

Call out, celebrate the beam
Imprisoning and expressing him.
Fix the mature flash for the end, but in advance
Fix in the glow of that sense what shall pass.

II

Give him a pale skin, a long hand,
A grey eye with deep eyelids, with deep lids.
Complete with a dark mouth the head
Of Veronese's equerry; though of too confident a grace
His gestures, less fine than his limbs. Allow him also to sleep much,
As with an effect of wantonness. Then he should swim and run,
Jump horses and touch music, laugh willingly and grow
Among plain manners and legalities, and yet,
Say where Monongahela and Alleghany
Have woven preparatives, glistening fall, or where
New York assembles brittle towers. And let him,
Pleased to accomplish purposes,
Alight in loose dress from a car.

III

He arrives thus with the ray of his intelligence
With what may cluster about it, dispositions
Recollections and curiosity, the state
Of reason and vision, the deceits of passion,
Play of reserves, reflections, admirations
I am luminously possessed of. And all of which am anxious
To acknowledge makes him another of the many-minded, another
Exposed and assaulted, active and passive mind,

Engaged in an adventure, and interesting and interested
In itself by so being. But here solutions bristle,
For the case seems to shine out at me from the moment
I grant him all the mind I can; when I in short
Impute to him an intemperate spirit, a proud wit
And in a springing innocence that still cannot undo itself
The pallid fire I cannot if I wish, withhold. He shall
As he does, overpraise and underprize
And outvalue and contemn all those purities and powers
Of sight and speech, the so true so rich fleece
Covertly and attentively, and often too
Fastidiously and rashly to neglect.
Here the position, action on his part, his going
In a still preserved uncertainty of light
Waits only for my touch: and there I have him
Amid the impunities of the polluted city,
I see him in the stale glare of those follies,
Illiterate illuminations run to seed,
Irreconcilables and abominables
Of all kinds swallowed, neither good nor bad
Either remembered or forgotten. In the dusk
There appears the full pallor of his looks,
Desiring and desiring to desire.
And in fine he proceeds, fanned by this dubious flush
In the way I know. It comes to me afresh,
There glimmers out of it upon me that I want
Nothing to come of it at once. It glimmers,
It glimmers from the question, of how, how shall it fall
The moment of the simple sight? and where
In what green land the simple sorrow? and
Under what boughs beneath whose hand wherever,
As in a fog upon the perfumed Cape,
A falling together of many gleams
Neither remembered nor forgotten, and neither
Undesiring nor desiring, the moment of despair?
Only say it should fall, as it will fall, as it fell
Or will have fallen, hanging back but to take place

All at once in the tacit air and on the ground
Of this period: the process
Of confrontation, reflection, resolution
That follows, it is this that will ascend
To the last point of fitted and related clarity.

IV

Caught in that leisurely and transparent train
Of the soft ostensibility of story,
His motions and his thoughts are their own net,
And while the beam folds on itself, I'll not
Deny it is indefensibly too fine.
For as in smooth seas under dawn, whatever
He does, he cannot do amiss
Being in these eyes seen aright
As he questionlessly is
In the white air under dawn
If he lives, if he dies
He but plays at all escapes
As a dolphin or salmon leaps,
And exquisite heresies
But leave the musing surface with a gleam.
So if all else be but conceivable, yet
Of a lucidity that lives, himself
Mirrored may be the same,
Antecedents and foils will palliate. For
How idly miraculous
Or of what tortuous glory,
In fact this creature was
How should my mere ingenuity relate?
In the great sweetness of which light
I ask if maybe I have made
Though in an ecstasy of loss,
At the last too little of it? But at least

Since I have seen him clear,
Whether he fondle a golden mare
Which he has ridden through wet woods,
Or in the sunlight by the water
Stand silent as a tree, this verse no longer weeps.

On a Cold Night

What mind lying open to my mind,
At a brazier crouching do I watch
A winter's night? Is it to find
Under the long night out of which
A full moon sallies and floats on,
If the wind knows what voyage it fails,
When the wind finds that she is gone?
A great gaiety filled our sails
For the adventure we were in;
The mercurial whisper fanned
Vainglory and discipline.
That mind lies open to my mind
And to the moon's eye. We decayed,
We decayed. And who knows
Whether her laugh says what it said,
What she wears and where she goes,
Or at the midnight of this night
And in the cold bed she will have,
Whether she weeps, having taken fright
At the thought that it is her grave?

The Intention

That at last the illustrious child
You, I would have said, would yield
Your locks of a light silk that's frayed
And eyes that had not yet betrayed.
And all the world would have known why,
Believe me, a day when the warm sky
Were colour of an oyster shell:
You and the world had seen as well
As I, when I reflected you
As looking on a dim clean view,
Or buttoned in a coat of grey.
And our abundance would obey,
I'd have said, what these eyes brought it,
Thought so, and you too would have thought it.

The Token

More beautiful than any gift you gave
You were, a child so beautiful as to seem
To promise ruin what no child can have,
Or woman give. And so a Roman gem
I choose to be your token: here a laurel
Springs to its young height, hangs a broken limb;
And here a group of women wanly quarrel
At a sale of Cupids. A hawk looks at them.

Words from Edmund Burke

To the vigilance of my exertions a lax pause,
Offering in the vehicle and wavering colour of evening
My weakness to my judgement, whether it may be a fault
Of defect or excess in me, or whether most
Not from a sort of habit of having what I say go for nothing?
For although I had allowed (I hardly shall allow)
That fable of persuasion, should I have no title to surprise
Upon felicitations of failure? And yet it is the time,
And I own as I ought to do, I have failed, I shall fail
Failing with the aid of all the images you may choose
For the proprieties of sentiment and the canons
Of a liquid eloquence; of links
Of favouring lights, of medals, of hinges, my grammar
My logic, vocables like faggots, triple cords, gongs, florets
A whole chivalry of leaves: I mean
An inordinate number of decorated reflections branching
Into how many more I have hinted at, as well as joints
Fans and ligaments and horns. I am an artisan of fire.

Far as this our business bearing me, thus far am I led to set
My ripe steps on a way I see before me, a soft pace
That tests it as to the use I may be of in the sorrows we
Have seen too much of. But since the times
Will come to worse: and neither the senate nor the soldier, not seeing
As I do, great London like a fuscous rose, her door-ways
Warm with the flux of quality, her shops bundles of muslin sown
        with rubies,
Her frigates tilted above the mud at low tide, and the town
Like a heap of fresh wet stars; and neither
The mushrooms of her markets, nor her polity nor her pravity
Will observe the secreted city of the speaker: let then this
Be to the other a sepulchre. Advanced I have my city,
And under the glimmering decadence of heaven, deepened,

Displayed the broad and dividing streets, the close columns
Of a sea-stone, the straitened palaces, the shallow quadrants
Vacated theatres, full graves and the temple trembling
To the least word. And I have watched it,

And in vain. And in vain before it I have turned
Too completely the religious animal. My thought, sight,
And what I saw a song; my instruments must intricately
Simulate an involuntary ascension, melt in flight.
And that austere insolence of tune was (nowhere near
The loud grudge of levellers) a manner of grovelling
To some tyranny of snow at morning. And all
To be connected it may be with the fact
That I came once from abroad, bred
In a transmarine province, whence
The more my eyes, my tongue the more might
Cling to the forms I have laboured to obtain; and so,
All the constructions put upon what I would be at, in that I would
Drink with my own looks, touch with my own hands, were
Eminently subject, being of a soft rash love
To the defamations of boyish fates, and the rudeness of those who
would glory
In a revolution of things. I hope I

Am as little awed out of my wits by the fear
Of vulgar shrewdness, as most of those I esteem. I have neglected
To follow, to bow to fortune. Yet if I love, I may lie:
And if I shine, obloquy will have it as a serpent
Who's in love with how he shines. And of a truth there is
This of wonderful in it that I should then
Prove no stronger than my passion: the machinery
Is itself well enough to answer all ends,
Were the matter but as sound; but what will serve
The arrangement of rottenness? Why should I build
With pain, were it with honour, and besieged by much foul gold,
On such frail stuff as the state? Why for an art
The lowest choose, choose also to revive

What other men no longer would believe? But so I must:
The fire that's born of peace returns to peace,
No phoenixhood resides in a transparence;
I should have died into the death I saw. And so I choose,

And to undertake the odious office of a priest
Among a diseased and desperate people, prosperous urchins
With the condescension of a conscious victim visit. Suffer,
Restore the flown thing. Sorrow with palms
Would 'fallen fallen light renew'. So I rejoice
To resign the lustres of a true success,
Myself to be what I pursued or praised, and so delight
To proclaim that cunning agony of rectitude, that my actions
Shifts and equivocations, all were and will be answers
To an immense mass of dark dealings. The system stretching now
To tracts that will be rank in future ruins, in both worlds
There is now this fistulous sore that runs
Into a thousand sinuosities; and the wound now
Opens the red west, gains new ground.

What disarray of an irresistible weather damps the fag-end
Of our day? And I bear it like a girl.
I am afire with its tears, my words have the asperity of tears,
I am it would seem an acceptable tube; and therefore
While time is, let me be used.
And therefore not the miserable managements,
It is not the infringements on dusty plains
Of a corrupted oriental cavalry, it is not
The caballing of the monied men, and not
The refuse and rejected offal of strolling players, nor the hazards
Of a den of outlaws upon a doubtful frontier nor even
My own colloquies at dawn with deploring fields,
Will seduce me (I hope) or silence me. I hope my unhappy blood
And its favourite fever may be given the grace
To give the truth my voice, truth to my voice, and may
The rich web so establish, while words are, while time is.

To a Friend on his Marriage

A beautiful girl said something in your praise.
And either because in a hundred ways
I had heard of her great worth and had no doubt
To find her lovelier than I thought
And found her also cleverer, or because
Although she had known you well it was
For her too as it had once been for me
Thinking of her: I thought that she
Had spoken of you as rare and legendary.
Now again, hearing that you marry,
My insatiable sense of glory and
My passion for the gay and grand
Deliver you up to fiction. A beautiful
Girl might once have played the fool
If you had called the tune, and I would too,
If anything that I might do
Could ruffle up your rose or flush your glass.
Because you are all things, and because
You show the world the glitter in the face
Of that all-but-extinguished race
Of creatures who delight in and desire
Much less the fuel than the fire;
I wish that when you call for supper, when
You sit down, guests and serving-men
May seem light-bearers planted on the stair,
Lights in the roof, lights everywhere:
So that as if you were a salamander,
Your sensuality may wander
In a community of flames, and breathe
Contentment, savouring wine and wreath.

To My Sister

I said that you should stint your wit,
But you were right to answer
That seldom could a beauty sit
When born to be a dancer.

You are richest when you scatter pearls,
When with an eagerness
More like a sea-gull's than a girl's,
You make your voyages.

Go on, and with your wealth amaze
And still the watcher. No man
When she'd be so, as Balzac says,
Should interrupt a woman.

The Letter

Coming across a letter
That a year ago
I had laid aside to show,
When cloud and flame should scatter,
That what the writer's pain
At the loss of love
Had accused me of
Should prove to have been vain;
What am I now to do
When staring without tears
On those characters,
I find that it is true?

Keeper's Wood

Within these dusky woods
The blackthorn hides.
The violets in the rides
On a grey day
Among pale primrose-buds
Crouch, hidden away.

A loud jay curses all.
A gust goes by
Under the cloud-cold sky,
And as you walk,
In the fields the lambs call,
And the rooks talk.

How pale it is, the sky
That sheds its peace
On the violets like a fleece,
And yellow buds,
While the lambs feebly cry
Outside the woods!

False Bay

She I love leaves me, and I leave my friends
In the dusky capital where I spent two years
In the cultivation of divinity.
Sitting beside my window above the sea
In this unvisited land I feel once more
How little ingenious I am. The winter ends,
The seaward slopes are covered to the shore
With a press of lilies that have silver ears.
And although I am perplexed and sad, I say
'Now indulge in no dateless lamentations;
Watch only across the water the lapsed nations
And the fisherman twitch a boat across the bay.'

The Babiaantje

Hither, where tangled thickets of the acacia
Wreathed with a golden powder sigh,
And when the boughs grow dark, the hoopoe
Doubles his bell-like cry,
Spreading his bright striped wings and brown crest
Under a softening spring sky,
I have returned because I cannot rest,
And would not die.

Here it was as a boy that, I remember,
I wandered ceaselessly, and knew
Sweetness of spring was in the bird's cry,
And in the hidden dew
The unbelievably keen perfume
Of the Babiaantje, a pale blue
Wild hyacinth that between narrow grey leaves
On the ground grew.

The flower will be breathing there now, should I wish
To search the grass beneath those trees,
And having found it, should go down
To snuff it, on my knees;
But now, although the crested hoopoe
Calls like a bell, how barren these
Rough ways and dusty woodlands look to one
Who has lost youth's peace!

The Moonflower

The secret drops of love run through my mind:
Midnight is filled with sounds of the full sea
That has risen softly among the rocks;
Air stirs the cedar-tree.

Somewhere a fainting sweetness is distilled.
It is the moonflower hanging in its tent
Of twisted broad-leaved branches by the stony path
That squanders the cool scent.

Pallid, long as a lily, it swings a little
As if drunk with its own perfume and the night,
Which draws its perfume out and leaves the flower
The weaker for its flight.

Detached from my desires, in an oblivion
Of this world that surrounds me, in weariness
Of all but darkness, silence, starry solitude
I too feel that caress—

Delicate, serene and lonely, peaceful, strange
To the intellect and the imagination,
The touch with which reality wounds and ravishes
Our inmost desolation.

All being like the moonflower is dissatisfied
For the dark kiss that the night only gives,
And night gives only to the soul that waits in longing,
And in that only lives.

In a Province

Because of the memory of one we held dear,
Call to mind where she lived and the ruins there
Among the silken shrubs. I have dismounted where
Her children played, and watch the pale sky grow clear.

And as for me, standing between the silken shrub and the broom
And tasting the breath of the blue sage, I must stay
Though my friends are setting out with the first of the day,
And they murmur to me, 'Do not linger in that gloom;
Remember that tears make whole the heart.' But I say
'Is there nowhere I may rest among the shells
Of the ruins and the droppings of white gazelles?
However brief my hours are, I would delay.'

The tears that fall from my eyes have wet my hands
Holding the reins of my horse. How many hours
Were sweet to me because of women! These showers
Bring to my mind that day among pale sands,
Call to mind how one came with me unwillingly
On an evening warm as another country's noons,
And all seemed of long ago among those dunes
And under a clear sky, under a clear green sky.

Chapel-at-Ease

The ceiling is carried on corbels laid
In the spandrils of the arcade;
Gold-leaf laid upon stone, the gilded stone
Is cut into a small pavilion,
Where when the town is still
The mind wills mind to will:
And at the level of the string
Triple shafts to the ceiling spring,
The spandrils being filled with tracery
Under the clerestory: the clerestory

Having a window of two lights
In each bay. Watching many nights
Shall I see her enter into her Chapel-at-Ease,
Chapel Pleasant, the chantry of her peace?
She delays, and who but I,
Who but I can tell why
The empty chamber shines? You see,
It is hers, though it is not she:
And the singing statue's open mouth professes,
Though not for her, what stone her being blesses.

She will not come, she is sitting where
Her friends are. Twilight fills the air,
Now and then she will look up to the sky.
Here under the planet-painted canopy
Voices of women, of boys
And men, promote sweet noise:
Till one comes calling out of hell
Like the clapper of a crazy bell,
And cursing like a drayman or a whore,
His house is burning, the whole world's at war.

For the Deserted

The mind, an irremediable virgin
Dabbles me in these vagrancies and forces
Others to do their harshest, to deflower, to deprive
His absence of my patience. The rough hedge
Perfumes my fierce infamies, or of a sudden
A twice desolated solitude (that's I)
At a thought breaks into broad wounds that remain,
Or at his touch in thought, open again.
Haunting the innocent green desert I'll seek
His essence hidden in some thin tent, and cry
'If I die, what will you do?' but what I have wished
Be the wilderness I have and that he gave.

For Fugitives

For you who loved me too
As the mistress of transparent towns that showed
Like sea-beasts the embodied ruins
As their bones, it is I who loved you
And crossed the sea, the flawed air
Allayed, now feel beneath my fingers
The seal melt from the fountain,
And recall the lost palatinate.

And for you whose it was
Who can forgive me? what may I offer? as
On this the other shore, unless
A dream rehearses loss,
Air of its charity will flush, the thin moon
From the white kernel of her filmy almond
Leans, and a causeless radiance fills
The palm I dip among these hills.

For Thieves and Beggars

On the plain is a tower
For robbers, with a grey wall where
A tattered sentry leans upon his pike,
And but the pious viper dwells: but you
Who are gone we also who
She and I here wander, we
Not refuse to remember, and all of you.
And the wall melts,
The boughs toss, the rocks
Nod overhead at nightfall while
We see all things as they might be.

And moving how slowly we two now
Know we are gone from those hills where
(Who cares in what full year?)
In that year all was pure,
To the hollow belonging to so
Few wings, and those half cold,
To which we sang. And for our voices,
None could aloud more loving do
Than when prolonging terminations we
Ourselves in our voices
Captured, caressed, and freed.

So we who in love at this hour
Walking as dumbly as beggars,
Cover the shabby moor and use
The blind shells of cracked houses,
We who no longer matter go

Against a veil of voices dying
Into the voices of
The dead a virtual twitter, seeking
A naked word we find
A dead man lying on his back
Under a sooty tree. He went in want.

Cefalù

These softs and solids, this clear, that rough,
Join, not long after dawn, in willing peace.
The blue hollow not stirred by the seed of a breeze;
A fallen marble block, the cape: the sea
Not stained by a gust or submerged shower holds glassed
On its woman's face no warning of a cloud.

The rocky front on which I lie
Bares to the play of early light
Its traces of invited wounds, a soldier
Resting, and with his helmet lifted back;
Dew on his cheek has left its torn white threads.

Some tide has sunk from us, not only the night;
The damaged sails and oars have sunk, the battle is snuffed.
The visitant steps no longer from the sky;
Her house is long broken, younger ramparts crumble, harness rusts.

This calm yet deceives: it is
A weariness of too much strength
Smoothes itself over with a polished care.
Such peace a balance built of ardent powers,
Such fetters are detachment; as if a love
Had prospered, dropped in breathless sleep, and two
Left by the darkness in each other's arms
Were lying, ignorant of all but self.

Some want there is, while blood still moves.
Though at a whisper should the never-twice minute flee,
A voice once locked in the ground, as in me, or closed
Under sea, or washed to air, should come, should cry,
Insisting in a song we are not dead.

For to keep the shining water is but one way;
To have the stone, but one; to own the air,
But one: and drowned or broken, rotted away,
I should not need these lover-like pretences.
But the day will not blind me, the silence not make me deaf,
And solitude it seems will never kill,
Though bedded with solitude; my breath is still here.

So, since we live, we must speak. Themselves
These friends dissolve their truce. Each again breathes,
Again knows the others and himself. The flood
Slowly with trails of a wing is striped:
One rush of freshness poured like silk frays out
Its winding fringes in a circle, one
Chases off from side to side with varying force.
Bands of these light persons brush—
Gathering rumours, furtherers of quarrels—the headland's height.
Blades and tongues and minute fins of wind will
Combine to dapple with cool the molten field,
And crisp the heavy flattened swathes of watery hay.

The eastern sun beats nearer, the dew dulls,
Falls or flies; and cloud like a suspected coast of hills
Drives up, procession of silver rocks, and I
Rise, trembling, stretch, struck to the bone
By the glitter of a fire-and-water world.

Chaka

I THE KING WATCHES AT NIGHT

The air cool and soft,
The darkness early about this sorrow, I
Am alone awake, I am alone
To watch the trembling of so many tears
Above my hard and empty lands. The plain
Mutilated and scarified, with dust and ashes on a black face
Looks brittle as a moth's wing. Shall I weep?

The cattle had been gathered in the village, the leader
Bellowed on two dull notes, when
Passing a poor woman's hut I sniffed her hearth of curds and
    embers,
At dusk under the grey smoke of a dung-fire.
I heard her call her babes to supper and saw
The too-big-bellied urchins
Come clustering to the porridge-pot. And I thought
'You have done well for yourself,
But it is not very long
Since you would run weeping home because of the thunder,
When the storm threw the old trees on their chins.'

Often night lets down darknesses upon me,
And every kind of doubt to weigh upon me. Then
I have said to him, as he thrust out his breast,
As he leapt forward like a pitch-black bullock,
As he buttocked with his buttocks,
I have said 'Night,
Are you not coming to an end because of dawn?'
And he murmurs back, the night,
'You go too far, you have gone far enough.'

I have wandered out in the thin tang of white stars
While my friends were asleep below the hills.
Depending only on rumours of my starry meals,
It was not for them to know how far my gaze was set.

II He Compares Old Customs with Those
of his Kingdom

There would come up many idle men to sit with the strangers
And sit down at our side. How they puffed off their words!
They would ask us what ancestry we were of;
We would tell them that, and tell them
How for our ancestors we set apart
A bit of a broken pot, or a forked stick
It might be, in the hut, or a little shrine
As who should say, a set of stones
Carefully selected, with a tree growing up in the middle:
Or how there might be a special sacred tree or grove of trees,
Or finally there might be a true tomb
Used as a temple.

The variations might be innumerable,
But there would be always remembrance,
It would be always as we said,
Although the manner of our remembrance varied:
There might be libations of beer,
There might be gifts on those altars
Of all that men use for food;
There might be prayers and appeals from those in trouble.

And they replied, and they said
'We think well of these men,
Who it seems will be far off on some high place
Perhaps, by the day dawning.'
And they made us sit down again
To hear again how we reverenced the dead,
And filled up our pipes with sweet herbs
Although they had not half enough for themselves.

But now the old men and the infirm have been well killed;
Now there are spies who crawl back from the south
Bearing on cheeks and shanks the sores

Of a new sickness. They will be burned. And there are captains
Who have returned from failure, to be hanged.
And my singing messengers have taxed the coast,
My soldiers weep with hurry at my commands:
They go out to slay, they return at night weary of slaughter,
They advance and attack and outflank and flee, all at once.
And on the most desirable of my hills,
In the sweetest of fastnesses, I speak well of them.

And I have divided the captives, allotted them ranks.
From time to time thus I established
Twenty-five regiments.
Some wear a headdress of otter-skin, others of leopard-skin,
The wing-feathers of the eagle or the ostrich
Are commonly added to these,
But the red wing-feathers of the green lory
Are worn only by royal grant.
And I have given them names,
Called my regiments Decoys,
Slashers, Gluttons or else Bees,
Ambushes, Mountains, the Blue Haze:
So we had too a name in the world
And war was our host in these places (there was blood in the dregs
         of the cup).

And so with white or black ox-tails, kilts of leopard-skin
And the broad shields of stretched cow-hide,
White or brown with a crimson or with a black spot,
They went out. So my state
Was fanned by a frond of fern, and in the red shadow
Of cloud-like trees I was repaid.
Among gossip of moist leaves, tongues of an upstart court,
To my gaudy establishment as general
Many emissaries, bitter, brought the crane's feather,
And offered many tokens to placate, including
Sea-shells and a quantity of melons.

III How Festivals were Celebrated

The eyelid severed from its terrible schemes
Is reproached by a leafage built of numberless small flames;
Tenderness is peculiarly active
In the first days of spring weather.
The province is all astir with fronds and buds,
And when one walks out in the meadows a sweet steam
Floats up beneath one's foot. A scarlet tree
Lit by the late wet season to her tips,
Sways and offers to the man who sways a scarlet crown;
And shakily a man's mind
Controls its longing to be spilt,
A couple of dew-drops lying
In the hollow of a leaf.

So a man may be slain for his eminence in dancing,
When the plain is alive with hair-like flowers!
And at last there will be something to be said
That I have made my own.

I have brought fear to this people,
I have rendered them as rich and smooth as ox-blood:
But am I a bird of prey, that I pursue
Only after the scent of a carcass? I might say
How with my lust I have refreshed the laws,
Giving out orders to hoe; and in the autumn
How some were allotted new wives;
How after my hunting they passed many hot days
Tossing the meat the one to the other
And laughing at the fat that hung in tassels.
The condemnation of the warriors at an end,
Those who might die with the chief I kissed on the breast and
    dismissed.

And there were the high days of the mind, the days of high feasting,
There were the feast days when, bare as a bolt

I danced before the people: as, on a dumb waste of green grasses
And lilies tangled like a sheep's wet back,
When the dawn's light was snowy in the sky and underfoot,
Light bubbled up and trickled to my foot. And on an evening
Wreathed with fond hues when the red rock
Smoked with a soft flame it had sucked,
And when the washed air with that flush
Was burdened, I might have cried I was puffed up
With gross and fanciful enjoyments. Holidays
When on the smooth floor of a public place
As if in the teeth of all things I would act
As thunder, commandeer an echoing tube
And a congratulatory drum. And there were days
When the young sky was like a lake, but softer,
And to my voice, to purify the army,
The rivers once down, to depart in the dust
Of a perfumed month, a month
Of pollen, we devised a long dance before bathing.

IV   HE BATHES IN THE MORNING

Wings rise, the shrubs flutter.
I have bathed in this solitary water,
And by the pool beside the flowering thorn
I turn a question over in my hands.
And in the opinion of this palest empty dawn
When a couple of birds to mock are making apart a single song,
Which of us can forgive himself? for all are,
The song says, guilty of all.

The odour of journeys mingles with despair.
If the branches of the sweet-thorn are all broken,
They have been broken for our sins. Yet everywhere
The sweet-thorn with an odour
Of honey pains the deep waste of this hour of penitence.
The male bird gives a whistle,
And his companion caps it like a bell;
And there is only this, that we are worthy.

V THE PEOPLE REST AFTER CONQUESTS

Such were the gifts inflicted upon us who trembled
At their brilliance. And a sharp rain
Having poured, we stretch ourselves in the sun to heal.
The hills are like old men sitting in their blankets,
The wild things are gay. Buck jumps, hawk dives.
And at the tip of that peak, like a knot
Of white spittle in a brown pool, see, that cloud
Softly clinches peace. The deepest colour,
The most mysterious, that of our flesh, tells
We have eaten luminous shadows. We smoke hemp,
And the conversation of some swallows is both a keen burden
And sweeter than that of the dead. And the foot-hills grow rosy;
A leopard-skin is trodden beside the enraptured river,
And stretched on the glossy backs of boulders. The woman is
          panting,
Her dugs hang forward as she leans; as for her daughter,
She is light and dreadful as a spear, she too leaves a gash.

We clap our hands together. What do you dance,
What do you dance? we ask. We clap hands. How
Is it one sings your king's name? We have dreamed
Of an adorable authority, and the brooks
Sobbing absurdly in the bright morning, the brooks
Glitter. There is so often news,
Yet we listen for news of the Men of the Sun, and of the Mist,
We murmur against the Men of the Baboons and those of the
          Showers,
We learn of the Men of the Little Bluebuck, the Men of the Young
          Lions,
Of the Sons of the Dancers of Iron, and of the Children
Of the Elephant. All these are ours,
And we are the People of Heaven. Tell us no lies
On our noons made loud by abolished clans.

Soldiers Bathing

I

Soldiers Bathing

The sea at evening moves across the sand.
Under a reddening sky I watch the freedom of a band
Of soldiers who belong to me. Stripped bare
For bathing in the sea, they shout and run in the warm air;
Their flesh worn by the trade of war, revives
And my mind towards the meaning of it strives.

All's pathos now. The body that was gross,
Rank, ravenous, disgusting in the act or in repose,
All fever, filth and sweat, its bestial strength
And bestial decay, by pain and labour grows at length
Fragile and luminous. 'Poor bare forked animal,'
Conscious of his desires and needs and flesh that rise and fall,
Stands in the soft air, tasting after toil
The sweetness of his nakedness: letting the sea-waves coil
Their frothy tongues about his feet, forgets
His hatred of the war, its terrible pressure that begets
A machinery of death and slavery,
Each being a slave and making slaves of others: finds that he
Remembers his old freedom in a game
Mocking himself, and comically mimics fear and shame.

He plays with death and animality;
And reading in the shadows of his pallid flesh, I see
The idea of Michelangelo's cartoon
Of soldiers bathing, breaking off before they were half done
At some sortie of the enemy, an episode
Of the Pisan wars with Florence. I remember how he showed
Their muscular limbs that clamber from the water,
And heads that turn across the shoulder, eager for the slaughter,
Forgetful of their bodies that are bare,
And hot to buckle on and use the weapons lying there.

—And I think too of the theme another found
When, shadowing men's bodies on a sinister red ground,
Another Florentine, Pollaiuolo,
Painted a naked battle: warriors, straddled, hacked the foe,
Dug their bare toes into the ground and slew
The brother-naked man who lay between their feet and drew
His lips back from his teeth in a grimace.

They were Italians who knew war's sorrow and disgrace
And showed the thing suspended, stripped: a theme
Born out of the experience of war's horrible extreme
Beneath a sky where even the air flows
With *lacrimae Christi*. For that rage, that bitterness, those blows,
That hatred of the slain, what could they be
But indirectly or directly a commentary
On the Crucifixion? And the picture burns
With indignation and pity and despair by turns,
Because it is the obverse of the scene
Where Christ hangs murdered, stripped, upon the Cross. I mean,
That is the explanation of its rage.

And we too have our bitterness and pity that engage
Blood, spirit, in this war. But night begins,
Night of the mind: who nowadays is conscious of our sins?
Though every human deed concerns our blood,
And even we must know, what nobody has understood,
That some great love is over all we do,
And that is what has driven us to this fury, for so few
Can suffer all the terror of that love:
The terror of that love has set us spinning in this groove
Greased with our blood.

                                These dry themselves and dress,
Combing their hair, forget the fear and shame of nakedness.
Because to love is frightening we prefer
The freedom of our crimes. Yet, as I drink the dusky air,

I feel a strange delight that fills me full,
Strange gratitude, as if evil itself were beautiful,
And kiss the wound in thought, while in the west
I watch a streak of red that might have issued from Christ's breast.

The Inn

February is the shortest month, and good
For this too, that we shall be one
With the campaigning season, and that done,
If I go where I would not by the way
I would not, on my journey I may say
That as it was, it will be; and I should
Come back the way I would to where I would.

Royal marriages were celebrated so,
Before the year's intrigues began.
A royal woman and a man
Were joined like puppets to beget a love
Imputed by the plot, and set to move
Apart, together, as you come, I go
To the unknown the way I do not know:

That's in your arms, where now you know, and why,
The war will happen for this year,
And we between us get and bear
Whatever is to be when we have been;
That you may not be but the winter-queen
Of schism in Bohemia, nor I
Elector of an exile where I'll die.

With politics like these the war uncharms
Our new-born marriage, that must learn
Such days as these that now return,
Are torn, and are to tear us. O but first,
We will lodge here: the weather may be curst,
But here's the inn; no manger but my arms,
Where none but you or I can do us harms.

The Dice

Were we not then, before we were
Made up in the one mind,
As if tied to uneasy beds, to stir
And argue with ourselves? As heretics,
Or disbelievers in religion find
A hundred reasons, each of a new kind,
Against the thing at which love sticks;
And all their subtly-shifting tricks
Were summed up if they said 'It is not true':
So half-aware of some adultery,
Even before we came
To be contracted one to the other, we
Half-loved, and thought love lame.
I in my madness found a way to be
Chimerical yet catastrophic; she
Was lost in an unending dream of me.

For I know now how she
Was, long before I knew
Her: as she recreates all things for me,
We make up all between us, and the skies
Are living in us, all we say or do
Marries them to the world, and through us two
Like needles in a haystack, and our eyes,
Such reasons and realities
Come singing like a fire, the truth comes true.
We are like a pair of dice that the soul throws
In this two-handed game—
Rattles the little box where the luck grows;
And it is all the same
Whether a six by six or six by four
Lies, or a five by two, or three, or more:
We add that to this, this to that, and score.

The Diamond

Must then all human love,
To those who come back from the desolation
Of seeking God in prayer or meditation,
Seem easy as the drawing on a glove?
For so it might have been,
That having contemplated heaven, we
Should afterwards know better what we mean
For being earlier baffled: find the seen
By what we never saw, yet brought to be
Worlds upon worlds in our two one, made one by you and me.

But to tell what, before
We came to be from chaos, or how we were,
When first I you, you me, began to stir
And struggle to make live, would but the more
Perplex and knot the tale.
Not in the marriage of such opposites
As you and I were, might we hope to sail
Through our Symplegades; yet when your gale
Has blest my flagging rig, above there sits
The spirit of the quarter, pipes, and so the vessel flits.

Thought's wreck gave back love's function.
What was the abstract that I made of all
Life, but the ledge where love, crouched, at a call
Sprang out in this improbable conjunction?
That diamond was the rock
From which the ship that foundered rose in the air
With all its canvas out and up, to block
The great wind with its wall—drive on the shock
Of foam-sheaves at its neck, and ride and bear
As long as winds and waters are, how far we can and care.

The Book

Now wars and waters, stars
And wires, the dead hand in the iron glove;
The bolted winds that ride death's cars;
Guns, gallows, barracks, poles and bars;
Seem to have laboured but to fetch us love.
Planets that burn and freeze
Now wring their hands, or forced to please,
Must twine them in a dance instead:
Distraught cosmogonies
Like bad old baffled fairies stand,
Where we, your head upon my hand,
Or sleeping hand in hand, or head by head,
Have closed the book of the day, and gone to bed.

But body, now be deep:
Worn hornbook, *Mirror of the Sinful Soul*,
Or *Abbey of the Holy Ghost*, *The Keep
Of Spiritual Valour*, keep
Your foxed and wormed and rusty pages whole,
That we may read our way.
Like an old lantern by whose ray
We hope to find a better light,
Glow feebly as you may;
Be torn and tattered, interleaved,
One chapter will not be achieved,
Until we read by touch as well as sight,
And learn to turn the pages, kiss and write.

You are periphery;
And we would be the centre, if we could
But break your circle, or could be
Without you, inconceivably
Ourselves our multitude and solitude.

You would be nothing then,
As now all other things and men
Are turned to nothing at a touch
Of hand or lip; again,
We'd seek the soul, and having passed
Through you and through ourselves, at last
Find the dark kingdom which denies that such
As selves, and thoughts and bodies, matter much.

O *Encheiridion*,
O *Salutaris Hostia* in this kind:
Until that darkness comes, be all-in-one,
Be shadow to our double sun,
But single, as the purpose of our mind.
For if by love we mean,
To seek and find a go-between
Spelt from your incunabula,
And see at length what can be seen
By some new light beyond decay:
Through you we must burn time away,
And wither with the force of our idea
The world of visible phenomena.

The Question

And so we too came where the rest have come,
To where each dreamed, each drew, the other home
From all distractions to the other's breast,
Where each had found, and was, the wild bird's nest.
For that we came, and knew that we must know
The thing we know of but we did not know.

We said then, What if this were now no more
Than a faint shade of what we dreamed before?
If love should here find little joy or none,
And done, it were as if it were not done;
Would we not love still? What if none can know
The thing we know of but we do not know?

For we know nothing but that, long ago,
We learnt to love God whom we cannot know.
I touch your eyelids that one day must close,
Your lips as perishable as a rose:
And say that all must fade, before we know
The thing we know of but we do not know.

II

Apollo and the Sibyl

Thyme, tufa, sage, anemone,
And we heard that music singing:
The sea, the heavens, and all rivers
Standing still to listen, the bare mountain
Bulging in delight
Rose hugely to heaven, dark grey lump uplifting
Height on height—
Up crags and winding levels,
Up paths and pathless rocks, to the bald crown
Stamped down by the winged hoof:

Clear water gushes from that blow;
Voices of those who are to die sing, shuddering.

I

—White sunlight and the dripping oars!

Capes naked to the north wind, and besieged
By honey-coloured poesy—
What was it I refused, refusing love?
'It was the vision of the light
From which I am shut out.' And what decided it—
What had I then desired, or hoped or feared,
To give or to receive?—Strange agony,
To stare on my disgrace through the soft spring!
But I reply 'I cannot know,
Because I cannot love, I only know
One need not taste some joys to know their sadness.'

Sad sapphire, much as cloud
Drizzles on glass-grey waters.
'And are you sad, and are you satisfied?'
'I am sad, but I am not satisfied.'
Gold eagles hover in the grey,
Goats climb up crumbling gypsum . . .

—And I was sad to lose that virgin sadness!
Alas, why had I fled from the reality? . . .

Look, you have disappeared, and now
Asphodel breaks grey stubble.
How do we know what will happen, who will tell us? . . .
And even now that faded radiance
You knew unfaded, shines; I am not yet much withered.

Therefore a thousand doubts, a thousand questions,
Most of them with no answer; as, I wonder
'Why did he not then force my love?' add suddenly
'You should have loved me more, why did you not?
You might have saved me.'

—Questions of hope, despair, changes of mind. . . .
Acceptance of the changeless mind!
And now I sit and hide my face;
And know that where the soft and rough tide hurries,
The tide will rise and wash the rocks tomorrow;
That cloud of an angelic dignity
Will form and melt tomorrow—and tomorrow,

While far out in the milky straits
The black shape of a boat sits,
And drags itself. . . .
Wet flashes on dipped oars.

II

Then came a time of great guilt, that I inhabited
Under the night's dark face
                              Declivities
And diamonds, high sorrow
                              Solemn tears
Trembling but never falling
                              Night

We watch you, brute white stars,
Panelled in brilliant silence, pendulous jewels
That rotate or pause
Quivering, hovering over us,
As if aware of the abyss,
And glistening like a forest of pale eyes:
The utter quiet of these skies
Dumb, gliding wildly aloof,
Wafted, glimmering with milky fires
Like thorn-trees hung with pollen, finches' nests
Of winged and torn desires,
—Furious and holy vacancy
Or tender dreaming fury, the pale jealousies
Of pity-breathing milk-stars,
And the crackle of dew-soft fire-drops
On great plains . . .

I walk alone, we walk on the dead world
Tied to our living heel, the whole wide sky
A kind of wild white living glimmer
Mirroring our lost nakedness.
The pallor and the sigh
Prepare a pure deep tomb where we
Might sole-survive to love, but see,
The gaping veil that fans our skin!
The pure desires take flight,
Leaving us naked, less

The vanished loveliness: the dusky tissue
Folds us in tragic opposites,
Bedaubs us in deliberate glitter,
A numberless dull dazzle, wretched glory...

Dim shams that grimly glimmer
And we abhor, abjure;
Dead thistledowns of bitterness,
Or withered plumes of nothingness
Suspended, the vast gestures
Of some frustrated exploit:
A distant dog barks, and the sombre shimmer
Shifts, bristles.
              And do we hope to regain
And gather softly, all shut up alive,
The shadowy body, the bare breast,
And dusk like nakedness and dew like darkness
Hung with the jewels of ourselves?

—Where the dark serpent glows,
Rising and slowly sinking
Through the starry murk, the noon of night;
Lonely to one alone it comes
Like that wild trembling permanent sky
That has divided us, and brings
The prison of these things, the terrible trembling,
And all that loveliness we canvassed! there,
The softness of those mirrored loins
Rises within my beating throat,
And then the taste dreams of some crust
Of what was lost, the starry meal
Of some delicious crumbled bread
Powdering all infinity; and then,
Love is the web, the bed
Soft-burning with religious breath,

For which the constelled waste, sage clarities,

Are brimmed with ghastliness of light
And echo silent cries of ours;
For only furtive love,
Known in the great fear, captive
Of the dire luxurious clarities,
Can find within our exile (damned,
Vituperated, loathed)
The sigh of peace, the delicate flight! . . .

The birds are silent in their nests. Black midnight,
And the crass blaze of our destinies but shudders
And utters nothing, only
Tracing slowly once again
The massive sorrow, the starred lineaments
Of silence and the infinite night.

III

The sky brims with the ghost of a great rage.

—I am alone, and on my height
The wind cracks and shudders,
Dust and sweetness whirl in the new light;
And washed in brilliant madness,
The whole coast glitters and expands,
Pale-brown to dull-red, off-white,
Capes and beaches laugh and clap their hands,

And the emancipated, wild and noble sorrows
Flash through the solitudes!
                              Like the sea-swallows
Swoop out and cut and glide, chafe joy and scud and skim,
Twittering drunkenly in flight
Their delicious scurrying music—dart upright,
Climb, totter, drop incontinently,
Grazing the low ground by the sea
And single brownish flower

Fast-rooted in the rocky soil,
The small sweet-scented broom
Whose tough stems bear a bloom
That is golden and subdued,
And significantly sad.

—And my dream and my despair,
My delight in what I hate,
My mourning, my desire,
Have wasted that estate:
And now a low brown person, shrinking slowly to a bag of skin,
I wonder at myself, and even more that, were I to begin,

I think that I should do what I have done.

And gulls, swallows, turn down wind,
The sea toils, grinds and crushes
Marble to milk at cliff-base.
                              And the air,
The air is stirring, everywhere
A sweetness dignifies the air:
The broom, that tanned and dusty angel,
Bound down, is taken by the hair
And rifled, and blown lingeringly, or plunged
By the wind's tooth and talon, torn
But living and enduring, the sweet doom
Like an imaginary face
Springs out of the rough shrub and floats in ambush,
To honey our disgrace.
                    —Each grain of dust or grain of gold
A universe of incense!...
                    And the birds and the birds' cries
Are blown about the empty plain and skies.

IV

And yet the Sibyl parches, caught and clutched within a fist of dust!

—Burning and ribbed abysses, broken cradles, empty shores
And the uneasy airy glitter, the slow glow
And then the massive flash
That answers irresistibly,
And sobs and rubs and woos,
Mirrors and writhes and rocks itself and sighs
And strives to glut itself with light:

Dust on the parched bluff, on the rock-cliff,
And ruined splendour on the sea:
And looking down on the yellow town,
All glowing like a sun or star,
And farther than if I were dead
—So far away it seems, so far—
Sunlight and moonlight mix like joy with pain,
So that I cannot tell you which;
I only know the burnished tarnished surface, stretched
Over the wide sea, rich
Stretched like a rustling mirror haunts the air,
Flutters the glowing gulf
—Supple and subtle, full of stirrings—
And the impatient flood of calm,
To suffer but the mirrored softness burns,

And longs to melt its shores! . . .

And sitting upon my rock alone, unrecognisable to myself,
Moving motionless to death, I see
That one must suffer what one sees,
Living what it is not and it is.
And as I live my centuries,
Rejoicing in my choice that was
Either of happiness or this,

As of terror or of bliss,
I sing 'And I may live like this,'
I am not blind, I sing and see,

As balsam trees weep gum, as leathery pods
Breed tufts of silk, as bees thieve honey and thrive:

My mournful calcined life
Half-eaten by desires,
Brimming with light and sorrow,
Yet I do not repent me;
I remain in my pain that is
A golden distance endlessly,
And with my head bent, and my eyes
That follow down and stare
As with a dreaming stare, I gaze
Until the noon that climbs the air
Troubles, makes more than ever now excessive
—Rubbed and ruffled, thumbed—
Outrageously more beautiful,
The burning young tumescent sea,

And the smoke-black stone-pine, wings wide on the hushed air,
Hangs over its own shadow, tilted:
Smouldering incense of the pine,
Under the noonday, over the dark pool, cool.

        —And the sky opens
Like a fan its vault of violet light, unfolding
A wide and wingless path to the impossible.

The Old Age of Michelangelo

Sometimes the light falls here too as at Florence
Circled by low hard hills, or in the quarry
Under its half-hewn cliffs, where that collection
Of pale rough blocks, still lying at all angles on the dust-white floor
Waits, like a town of tombs.
       I finish nothing I begin.
And the dream sleeps in the stone, to be unveiled
Or half-unveiled, the lurking nakedness;
Luminous as a grapeskin, the cold marble mass
Of melted skeins, chains, veils and veins,
Bosses and hollows, muscular convexities,
Supple heroic surfaces, tense drums
And living knots and cords of love:
—Sleeps in the stone, and is unveiled
Or half-unveiled, the body's self a veil,
By the adze and the chisel, and the mind
Impelled by torment.
      In the empty quarry
The light waits, and the tombs wait,
For the coming of a dream.

    * * *

The power with which I imagine makes these things,
This prison.
And while the dream stirs in the stone, wakes in its chains,
Sometimes I think that I have spent my whole life making tombs,
And even those are unfinished. And yet, chafing,

Sadly closed there, in a rich bare case
Of bodily loveliness like solid sleep,
One sees the soul that turns
Waking, stretched on her side as if in pain, and how she sees
Browed like the dawn, the dark world
—Like a sulky pale cold louring dawn—
Loathing her hope of fruit, the pure bare flank;
Or else one sees her sunk in rest,
Letting her worn head droop over her empty body
And the much-pulled breasts hang dry,
Fallen, with long flat nipples.

And there is always
Some victor and some vanquished, always the fierce substance
And the divine idea, a drunkenness
Of high desire and thought, or a stern sadness.
And while it rests or broods or droops,
There will be always some great arm or shoulder
To incur or to impose some heavy torment,
There will be always the great self on guard, the giant
Reclined and ominous,
With back half-turned, hunched shoulder
And the enormous thigh
Drawn up as if disdainful,
Almost the bare buttock offered.
There will be always
A tall Victory with beaten Age
Doubled beneath its bent knee, but ignoring
(The naked proud youth bending aside
His vacuous burning brow and wide
Beautiful eyes and blank lips) but ignoring
The sad sordid slave, the old man.

*   *   *

And now I have grown old,
It is my own life, my long life I see
As a combat against nature, nature that is our enemy
Holding the soul a prisoner by the heel;
And my whole anxious life I see
As a combat with myself, that I do violence to myself,
To bruise and beat and batter
And bring under
My own being,
Which is an infinite savage sea of love.

*   *   *

For you must know I am of all men ever born
Most inclined to love persons, and whenever I see someone
Who has gifts of mind and body, and can say or show me something
Better than the rest,
Straightway I am compelled
To fall in love with him, and then I give myself
Up to him so completely, I belong no longer to myself,
He wresting from me
So great part of my being, I am utterly
Bewildered and distraught, and for many days know nothing
Of what I am doing or where I am.

—Young green wood spits in burning,
Dry wood catches the flame: and I become now
An old man with a face like wrinkled leather, living alone,
And with no friends but servants,
Parasites, bad disciples puffed up by my favours, or else Popes,
Kings, cardinals or other patrons, being as for myself alone
Either a lord or subject, either with my gossips and buffoons
And clumsy fawning relatives; or towards you and such as you

Whom I adore, an abject:

Messer THOMAS

CAVALIERE
I am naked in that sea of love
Which is an infinite savage glowing sea,
Where I must sink or swim. Cold, burning with sorrow,
I am naked in that sea and know
The sad foam of the restless flood
Which floats the soul or kills, and I have swum there
These fifty years and more,
And never have I burned and frozen
More than I have for you,
Messer Tommaso.

*   *   *

Moon-cold or sun-hot, through what alternations
Of energy, long languor,
Periods of mad defiance, periods of fear, flight, misery
Cowering darkly,
Moon-cold or sun-hot, love that grips
Sun, moon, eternal hatred
Eternal hope and pain, packed close in one man's body,
And drawn, leaning to others.

And one other:

Grey eyes float in the dry light
That might draw Venus' car, moving at morning
Grey eyes through dry dark shadows, floating
Over the blocked ways, the despair,
And opening wide lids, irises
More starlike than the stars, purer than they, alive in the pale air,
Fire, life in thin dry air
Drawing the soul out at the mouth;

Beauty in triumph,
My defeat.

         *   *   *

—I am always alone, I speak to no one
But that shabby Bernardo, nor do I wish to:
Trudging up and down Italy, wearing out my shoes and life,
Toiling still to grow poorer, ugly, sad,
Proud, narrow, full of unfulfilled desires!

Yet I have come to Rome, rich in its ruins, and for the last time,
As if I made to cross a little stream dry-foot
That had divided us, and yet again, for the last time
My dream grows drunk within me,
And opens its great wings and like an eagle
Wild naked perfect pure, soars from its nest.
Almost I am persuaded, almost, that it is possible,
My love, like anybody's love, is possible.
My eye stares on your face, and my old mind
Soars naked from its cliff, and thinks to find
—Drunk with illumination as the sky itself is drunken
Or a dry river-bed with light—
The wild path to its thought, for all is passion
Here, even cogitation, and it climbs and clambers, floats and flings
And hovers, it is thrust up, it is hurled
Throbbing into the stillness,
Rapt, carried by the blissful air
Borne up, rebuffs and buffets
—Having hurled
The dead world far below it—
Stretches out long rapturous claws and wings,
Stiff as with agony, shakes as with tenderness
And dives and hovers at you, swoops and aches
To stun, caress

And beat you to your knees,
Clutches and clings,

—As if it would grow one with you and carry
Up the solitary sky
That strange new beautiful identity,
Where it might never fade or melt or die!
And many things
Are put about and taken up and spread abroad
About Michelangelo, poor old man, but when I
Come to you, I care nothing
For honour or the world, I only care
To look long on your face, and let
The dream soar from its nest. For do I know
Myself, what I should mean? I only know
That if I had those wings, not in a dream,
And I could open, beat those wings;
If I could clutch you in the claws of dream,
And take you up with me in loneliness
To the roof-tree, angle of heaven, vault
Of exquisite pale buffeted glare:
I should gain or regain
The heaven of that high passion, pallor, innocence
—I should gain or regain
The sole pure love, and fence it with my wings.

*   *   *

But my two eyes
Are empty, having wept, and my skin stretched
Like an old hide over dry bones, and my face
Grown flat and timorous, broken,
Loving or having loved this dream.
And the light fades from the sky, the dream dies in the stone
Slowly, I finish nothing I begin, and in my evening

Last torments and last light, torn hesitations
Between desire and fear, between desire and my disdain
—Emerging into dusky rooms, high halls, rich architecture
And the tawny roofs of Rome. For this love discovers only
The world's desert and death, the dusty prison
Where we have shut ourselves, or the sky shuts us.

Fades the light, and below there
I lie, an old man like a fallen god propped up.
My eyes close, and my head hangs,
Heavy as if with love-drink or with dreams,
And from my old thick swagging side
Pours forth a marble river. Overhead floats
A face, two brilliant eyes
That make the whole world pale,
Floating, and that great nobleness,
That great despising, of the mind
To which the beautiful is as the felt heat
Of the fire of the eternal.

Do not forget the poor old man.

The Doors of Stone

Watching Song

I

Watch, I warn you,
By night and starlight,
You who are chosen to
Stand on the brick-built
Walls of Modena:
Wait for the dawn-hour.

II

Standing at arms and
Peering in darkness
Over the flatlands;
Pacing slowly
On open stretches
Of mortared levels or
Close in catwalks;
Pause and listen,
With lowered eyelid and
Heart under breastplate:
Question the silence.

III

—Nothing but frogs
That chatter in ditches,
And crying of nightbirds.
Yet we watch to
Outwit the sorrowful,
Shag-haired rabble of
Heathen raiders.

IV

And so in our sentries
Bound and helmeted,
Over the city
We sing our watches,
Call on the Name and
Summon our safety—
Singing in antiphon
Answer in unison
'Lord God omnipotent,
Shield and companion:

V

'Saviour and King
And crown of mankind;
You who were born for
Our peace, to stand over us,
Keep your hand over us.'

VI

Then, as the song goes,
Hear it echoing
Round by the walls
Of the guarded city,
Floating by tenements,
Roofs and courtyards,
Domes of churches and
Empty markets—
Stirring and comforting
Drowsy families,
Strangers at inns and
Close-laid lovers;
The patient candle
Of cellared workmen

Yawning at benches;
Shuttered taverns,
And prayers in silence,
And lamps by altars
That live in darkness.

VII

Then watch together, singing together,
And stand as faithful,
Hearing it echo
Round by the walls we
Keep in safety,
Until the first breath
Sent from the dawn-hour
Touches the night's face,
And the dawn brightens.

Cœur de Lion

Forbecause a prisoner lies
With no air or exercise
He has need, to save his health,
Of thoughts that will not give him grief:
I have friends of name and wealth,
But few of them have sent relief.

Ask what they have done for me,
Those who yet go rich and free,
All my barons, tall young men
Of Poitou, England and Touraine;
Once they were my friends, and then
They never knew me false or vain.

Much dishonour they may fear,
Should I lie two winters here.
Men and barons, they all know
Not one could be so poor to me,
I would let him stifle so
For want of money paid in fee.

Some may think my capture sent
As deserved, in punishment;
Others resting from alarms
Live unconcerned in heart or head,
Though the fields are bare of arms
And I do homage to a bed.

Not that I intend excuse
From the chance of war, ill-use,
Close confinement, fear and pain;
But this is over and above.
Of the others none complain,
But worse than all is loss of love.

'Moult sont Prud'hommes les Templiers'

Kings and Bishops murder law,
Yet we dare not complain.
Scholars wind a rope of straw,
Call it a golden chain.
Tired of these, and worse, I would
Be sworn a Templar Knight;
For that order seems all good,
Were they not bound to fight.

They have Golgotha to guard,
And keep the passage free
For all pilgrims, in regard
Of God, by land and sea.
Then, they are true knights and brothers,
No man keeps his own:
All must share alike with others;
So their love is shown.

Their great houses like their swords
Are strong and burnished bright.
Poor in heart and yet like lords
They live, to do men right.
Yet their order I refuse;
Their friendship, name and wealth
I would rather miss than choose
A battle, for my health.

Les Congés du Lépreux

Plague and sores beyond relief
Have pierced me, skin and bone.
I must set up house with grief,
And travel hence alone.
Death has forced me to content
And with a darkness buys me day;
Poverty has paid my rent,
And counts tomorrow for today.
Pity, with those two red eyes,
And sorrow, looking back on me,
Do these errands I devise
To friends whom I shall never see.

One who taught me how to write,
Gerard of Pontlouvain,
Pity, waft what I indite,
And weep, if it be plain.
What he taught me, now I find
Serviceable to my pain,
So beyond my scabby rind
I touch his friendship yet again.
Now there's nothing sweet or sound
Left about me, but my heart,
Sorrow, as you go your round,
Give him that, and so depart.

Those who catered to my woes
When I was going rotten,
Sorrow, thank, but also those
By whom they were forgotten.
They relieved my body once,
And gave it pleasure in their hour,
And the body I renounce,

But I would not be rude or sour.
Go and tell old Simon Hall,
Now that I peel from head to feet,
With his good men by the wall
I can no longer sit at meat.

Pity, you may say goodbye
To two more I shall miss,
Hugo and Bertyl, and thereby
Look pale, and tell them this:
They may sail for Palestine,
As I had done, and made up three.
With their cross they can carry mine;
The pagans have a truce, for me.
God has quit me of my vow,
I owe no ransom for release.
Say that I go with them now,
Although I die at home in peace.

The Stolen Heart

All the winter I have lain here,
And heard the big wind tug at the door,
And throb in the loophole, scare the mice
That scurry and pause beneath the floor;
And felt my heart leap up in fear
At every sound, and seen men's eyes
Wide in amazement when I start
And shudder, twitching arms and thighs.
For none of them can tell what heart
Should make me pale and moist with sweat,
Even to think of one good stroke
I gave in battle once, or met;
Or how in such a fear I woke
That day the witch came to my rest,
And with her bony hand laid bare
And stole the brave heart from my breast.
She took the knight's heart beating there,
And left me another, the heart of a hare.

I crawl to the loophole, peep with care:
The sun shines, pale blue hills are bare,
Bright rivers rush from melting snows.
One dark pine rises up beneath,
Where the black stork built last year,
And blue-black woods beyond the heath
Are overflown by rooks and crows.
And there I hear the hounds at bay,
So far, that I can hear and bear,
And follow the horn blown far away,
And quake in longing and despair.

Soon the swallows will return,
And wars begin again in spring;
My knights will ride out everywhere.
But I shall still lie here and mutter,
Until one day a swallow's wing,
Dashed in the loophole, turn and flutter,
And burst in a moment my heart of a hare.

Mortimer

March has flooded meadows,
Spring comes in a gale.
Ploughlands and bare hedges
Are bullied, and the pale
Gold willow-wands
Toss by the beaten ponds.

And now I am tormented
By such gap of loss
As this love can bring;
And the wind drops, and across
The russet lands,
Sad spring a moment stands.

Budding sweetness yet
Haunts that lack of breath:
The osiers and hazels
And alders flush in death,
And a bird cries
To open the dull skies.

Strambotti

I

What thoughts could ride or hover in my mind
Before we met, I cannot now recall.
You are the thread of gold I would unwind,
Until I wind it in a golden ball;
You are the gate that I must pass to find
My happiness, or find it not at all.
Therefore all other thoughts I had give place
To those good hopes I meet in your sweet face.

II

I am not lodged in such and such a street,
But live in banishment with dust and stones.
I wear these clothes you see for cold and heat,
And yet I burn and shiver in my bones.
Apparently I live, and work to eat,
But inwardly I die of wounds and groans.
And you know well that you can bring me balm,
My pearl, to whom I pray with open palm.

III

The god of lovers chose you of his race,
And for his house, and stayed when he was in.
So I sit down before your noble face
And scan it, mouth and eyes and cheek and chin.
No treasure could be found a better case,
That bears in writing what is rare within.
And so I read it on your forehead set,
And live and breathe, that I may have it yet.

IV

I wish there were a passage underground
That led by magic to your house and bed,
So I could be beside you at a bound
When I had made the journey in my head.
Then I should disappear and not be found,
And neighbours be persuaded I were dead;
But I should be with you in Paradise,
Where I could laugh, and kiss your face and eyes.

V

If I could seize that castle, hill and plain,
And have it compassed with a wall of glass,
And lead you in, and with a granite chain
Make fast the gates of adamant and brass;
When we were there shut up to entertain
Our love at leisure, no one else should pass,
But we in games and banqueting engage,
And never think of death, or grief, or age.

VI

If I could conjure shapes for you and me
I'd choose two living things that swim or fly,
Two fishes tumbling in a glassy sea,
Two eagles turning in a golden sky.
And in those shapes we should continue free
And still in love, until the sea ran dry,
The air failed, and the earth dropped in the sun,
And time was ended, and we two were one.

VII

One thing we have, but maybe as the seeds
That fell on thorny ground and could not grow.
One thing we have according to our needs,
Yet burs and briars may clog us as we go.
One thing is certain, and the way it pleads
Half sadly, telling us what we should know;
But that would do away with worse desires,
And bring us softly through a world of briars.

VIII

The kingdom of our love is like a tree
Grown from a little seed on level ground,
But now it stretches over land and sea,
And carries on its top an eagle crowned.
Below, a tent is hung for you and me,
Thick-set with rubies in a border round,
That says I came into the world to serve you,
And I may have your love, but not deserve you.

IX

Wanting more courage than a wandering knight
Led by adventures on from place to place,
Like him, if I should waver I do right
To gaze in silence on my lover's face.
For that pale oval shadow can make light
In my account, of danger and disgrace;
And if they were to come I would not yield,
If I could have it painted on my shield.

X

I'll take some wax and mould your likeness there,
Or roughly carve a figure out of wood,
And in my exile take it everywhere
And tell it everything a lover should—
My long desire, my constancy, my care,
And such bad thoughts as love may turn to good:
And think it is the sweetest thing save one,
Which is yourself alive, under the sun.

XI

The lover who could wear you like a cross
That gave a blessing to his neck or arm,
Might travel through the world and fear no loss,
Disease or danger, guarded by that charm.
A thousand seas and deserts he might cross
And climb up mountains, and not come to harm.
And I am safe from injury or spite,
If I have kissed you, for that day and night.

XII

Love and good luck breathed on the builder's hand
When he took thought and set the window so, ˙
And set it facing where the bed may stand,
And every day the sun will rise and show.
For when the sun is rising as he planned,
With it a gentle wind begins to blow
And darkness and the stars fade out above;
But your two open eyes are stars of love.

XIII

Who made this palace of so rare a stone,
Not to be daunted in a hundred wars?
For many came and wished it for their own,
But could not enter it with men and stores.
Why should it open when I came alone?
Yet I have passed, and shut the marble doors.
And being in, now I must keep the key,
For I'll have no one sharing it with me.

XIV

Counting the heavy days and heavy hours
I measure out the prison of this town,
And wear out stones with that desire of ours,
But not desire, by walking up and down.
And you are like a city full of towers
Set by a plain or river like a crown;
And you are like a sunset and a star:
But I am here alone, not where you are.

XV

I took my pen and added up the days
Dividing us, and meant my letter still
To tell you of my patience in delays,
And how it left me neither well nor ill.
But shining like the sun with fiery rays
That rushes from a cloud or climbs a hill,
You rose and filled the sky with such a bliss
That I could say no more, and sent a kiss.

XVI

And we are two, but neither tall nor short,
And equally in love in heart and mind;
And we are like two pillars of one fort,
Of equal faith and equally combined.
And we are two, but one in every sort,
If ever there were such among mankind,
And others who have wished, alive or dead,
To lie together in one grave, or bed.

XVII

I have come back, and find the empty street,
And house and window where our love was born,
Remembering how it came to be complete;
And linger, half in tenderness and scorn.
Who will remember where we used to meet?
Like us it will be crumbled down, or torn:
Dried earth be all of us, our love and pain;
This verse a tomb of pearl where we remain.

XVIII LETTER

Vanne, foglio gentil

Coming to write my letter, overcast
By all the days of absence that have gone,
I think of others passing as they passed—
So many days of sun that never shone,
Letters and days! And this is not the last,
And I must doubt, to see them stretching on;
And wonder then, why, if it would be strange,
Sooner or later, for our love to change.

And yet I know our luck has won the toss
So many times! and most of all that day
When your first letter came and chanced to cross
One I had ventured—half afraid to say
What I felt suddenly, in dread of loss;
And then your letter came, and in a way
Said less, but it could only be a sign! . . .
And so it all comes back, to breathe and shine,

And so I run it through, how love began:
The light encounter while we hardly thought
And pleasant company without a plan;
But then the wild desire, and we were caught.
How then we were afraid, and blight and ban
Had clawed at us like devils, but we fought
And in the end won sweetness from it all;
And how that would be sweeter to recall.

And surely we will call it up again
One day, and laugh to see it shine and sing—
Know it is not a dream, but true and plain,
And we shall never find a better thing!
Then we shall bless what we have bought with pain,
And close it like the two halves of a ring.
—Therefore my letter promises to go
And say, I wish that I could travel so.

Gregory Nazianzen

Sweet everlasting Love, daughter of God,
Whose dancing deluges the world with light,
Come down and sprinkle wild flowers on your way
And rain down moisture on our barren plains;
Enter the stony provinces of Greece
Where thousands of blaspheming tongues are loose,
And save us from their plague of babbling lies.

Come quickly, since for more than forty years,
Under Constans and Constantius, Valens, Julian,
What have we done but war on one another?
Bishops from Pontus, Media, Thessalonica,
Presbyters come from Africa and Italy,
Deacons from Paphlagonia, Crete and Syria;
Fronto the prefect of Nicopolis;
George of Illyricum and John of Trebizond
Encroaching, with Eusebian Antioch:
Flying about like beetles, meet in Councils
Eternal as the Caesars; where we all
Can now do nothing but re-write the Creed.
And now we can agree, and now it holds
Until we eat or sleep, or the wind changes,
And then we tear it up, recant it scoffingly—
Determine, and undo determinations—
Prohibit, and ignore our prohibitions—
Profit by ambiguities, form parties,
And angling in two Testaments for novelties
Maintain the edge of anger, but forget
The bread of angels, trodden into dust.

How easy with no scruples to exchange
These paper formulae! but how should we,
Who should be firm in virtue, sober, sure,

Not angry, if we are to teach, not blameable,
Walk with such policies? I should deceive
Neither myself nor God; and must offend,
If I should give an answer when men say
And laugh 'Where is your talent? Time goes on,
But you can show no increase'; and they say
'When will you ever speak, and make an end?
When will your light shine forth and show the way?'

My friends, why ask me when I mean to pay?
Surely the last hour will be soon enough, old age,
Grey hairs? For I am haunted night and day
By fearful thoughts, they bridle up my tongue,
And cramp me up and gnaw my bones and humble me,
    So that I cannot think of others,
    But only how myself can flee
The wrath that is to come—myself be free
Before I bid for others, and myself
Draw near, before I summon those afar.

Meanwhile in Asia in the very villages
Disputes are held concerning divine dogma,
The people standing by and taking sides.
    In shops and squares
Ask them the price of beans, and they discuss
The Ingenerate Word of God. In Alexandria
A crop of Jezebels run up and down,
Accounting it their grief and shame
The day they do no mischief. Ballad-mongers
Philosophise on things incomprehensible.

Yet always in the wicked Arian leaven
One sees intolerable, itching love,
Although frustrated and reversed to hate.
And while they struggle vainly to be free,
And long to murder what is strange and pure,
    Twisting upon themselves and tangled,

Writing from the thing they see,
They witness in their teeth to the one Faith
That we have kept and they cannot endure:
'Father and Son one substance',
And being consubstantial, co-eternal;
And in that single clause, the glimmer given
Beyond all allegory, carved in marble
Or like the breath of man laid up in Heaven,
We are uplifted into life and light,
Comfort in sorrow, hope in all uncertainties,
The rising up on those interior wings—
Enthusiasm, new desires, discoveries—
New tongues for the expression of new things! . . .

Drenched in the silver of old olive-trees
The little bay lies empty, in a trance.
I watch the far sea bathed in pale blue light,
And on the rough sea-wall the tone of time
Comes out, and on the fundamental rock
Scored over, lights and shadows pause and pass.
And there the memory of some one face
Yet living, some transparent thought at gaze,
And looking from deep lids where it had nested
As if it were a breath, a truce, a peace,
Safeguards our happiness, that is and needs
Nothing but a deep gazing on our love.

Campanella

The dungeon where they keep me is of rock,
Cut deep into the cliff below the ridge,
And here I have endured for seven years
Seven kinds of torment, seven times repeated,
And threatened with more pain a thousand times
And that I should rot here until I die,
Unless I make submission and recant;
And here I have pretended to be mad,
Setting my bed on fire, biting my fingers,
And calling this dull cell my Caucasus
Where I lie chained, and they torment me thus.
Now truly, Campanella, you are jangled,
The bell you tolled upon to wake the dead
Sounds now no better than an old tin can.

Sighs are my sustenance, my meat is groans,
Because I preached the Kingdom of the Sun.
And now I may remember what I saw
Out of this ditch of death, that I am here
For thinking otherwise than bats and owls
And blinding their old dens with too much light.
And now, my body lying on a bed,
Worn, meagre, bruised and broken, and my mind
    Filled with a wound-like sorrow,
I concentrate and meditate and find
All my old reasons as they were, their fire
    Lighting the golden world
Where I had argued things to my desire:
    It was a world
Of a luminous sea-richness where I saw
No more of yours and mine, or you and me,
But all things were in common; ancient law
Made new morality shine light as air,

And that white Lamb of Fate and Harmony
   Returned to triumph here on earth,
And every buried life came back to birth,
And all was changing or about to change,
And abject government re-born in brotherhood.

Therefore you tyrants, vultures, hypocrites
Schooled in our lamentations, now beware
The imminent destruction of your reign.
The day comes that shall slay your withered pomp
And tatter and confound your league of lies,
Unbind all captives, cast away all kings,
And gladden those whose angry hearts are turned
To greet God's chariot wheels. For the blind see,
The lame walk, the dumb speak and the deaf hear;
And all our ordinary ugliness
Grown stale and sour under the Law, our lives
Of black and vicious tincture, shall disperse
Like a dead puddle, and we shall be free.
   We shall rise and remain
   Out of the dust and pain
Of this detested idiotic world,
That dyes the white skin of our love with lust;
And drink the ray and perfume of the sun,
And cradled in its breath, taste when it glows
   Finite angelic sweetness
   Like a thought that comes and goes:
And we shall eat the bread of honest joy
And touch the sky-pale stone of nakedness.
The Most High comes, and will renew all things
In Palestine, where he will say and show
What every prophet, psalm and story sings.

But must I suffer here unendingly?
What, shall I never live and yet not die,
Although these pitiable slaves, my torturers,
Rub off on me their horrible desires

Until these walls are wet with faded blood?
Out of this depth I cry to you, my Lord,
'Just and true are your ways, O King of Saints',
And my tormentors who make flies of men
Must surely be degraded in reward;
Their stinks and noises shall become their pain,
While I am raised to some new happiness
From this unhappiness that kills me now,
And finding in myself a glowing gulf
Of effort and fidelity and fortitude,
Transfer my sorrow to eternal gain.

Yet all is closed, and like a kind of night,
As if to ponder some obscure dissent,
And tell me that the madness I enacted
Was no pretence, but only acted truth,
And leaves me now, and that I now am sane.
The fragments of my life by this no light
Look meagrely, and my desire again
   Roused in its bed of sorrow,
Has understood that all this is in vain,
And that the time will come when I repent.

Strafford

Fi à faute de courage, je n'en aye que trop.

I

Dark steel, the muffled flash
On iron sleeve and cuff; black storm of armour,
Half-moons and wedges, scaly wings and hinges,
Ovals and quadrilaterals and cylinders
Moulded in nightshade metal.

                  So he stands
With rod and sword of office, living fingers
Poised lightly on the sword-hilt, pale and still,

Wentworth, the black-browed Yorkshire magnate, with a rent-roll
Matched only by his pedigree, the long list
Of Norman-English quarters and alliances—
His patent granting D'Arcys and Despensers,
Latimers, Talboys, Ogles; Maud of Cambridge,
Quincy of Winchester; Grantmesnil of Hinckley,
Peveril of Nottingham, Ferrers Earl of Digby;
And crowned by John of Gaunt, Plantagenet.

And still the dark eyes gloom beneath the bent brows
As if impatient of himself, his greatness
Rooted in limitation, strength and weakness
Of fiery piercing mind, that wears the waning body;
And still resentful to be so resented
Pleads for his power and purpose, 'chaste ambition',
For 'power as much as may be, that may be power to do more good';
Yet as we read it further, pleads for pity:

'Pity me for the power that drives me onward,
Far from content and quiet, yet farther, wider, climbing higher,
Haunted by thirst and shadow, to slip the bar of shadow

Lurking within, but finding greater darkness—
Envy attending me, black clouds above the world's abyss,
Black streams that crawl below,
Envy, death's rivers.'

II

Old histories, pale, stained, yet beautiful,
Unfold from yellowing papers, tarnished print,
Their tales of times of trouble, fear and war,
Dry death and living love.
                              And still unsatisfied
Strafford lives on, he being of the kind
That are by nature never satisfied.

'Ever desiring best things, never satisfied
That I had done enough, but did desire
Always, I might do better . . .'
So he in sadness at the trial,
And long before, in letter after letter
We see the difficulty draw him on—
Not for the greatness only, but the difficulty,
And will to do what others will not do,
Well knowing what he does:
                              'I know, I know
And see the pinnacles I go upon,
Danger at every step, left solitary,
Left lonely in the heat of the day,
To bear it out alone . . .
                              'And so have reason
To carry my eyes along, and know that all my actions
Are cast into the balance, weighed and fingered,
And rubbed and tested whether gross or light';
And so defies them, flashing in despite,

'Content a' God's name!
So let them take me up and cast me down.
If I do not prove paragon, fall square
In every coign of duty to my master,
Let me perish, and may no man pity me!'

III

So to his master's work. And what a master!
Stubborn and yet irresolute, immovable
Always in wrong positions, only wavering in the right;
Thinking himself most gracious, but cold-hearted;
Cross-grained and peevish, far too fond of money;
Pleased as a woman with his easy cunning;
Anxious and yet self-righteous, self-justified
Yet sensitive to every rub or rumour.
—With that small elegance, that sad shut face,
Sullenly delicate, that wan mean dignity! . . .

Wentworth would have him King, uphold him King;
And for that narrow nature toiled and wrestled,
And had indeed upheld him for ten years
Caught in the closing circle of his rule:
Governing like a king away in Ireland—
Faithfully drawing odium on himself, the distant servant,
From sharking lords and lawyers—dealing justice,
Planted and dug and watered, pruned and fostered
Till the poor cried 'Never so good a Lord Deputy!'
And the King's purse was filled—to fatten courtiers.

IV

But to subdue two Kingdoms, distempered by their bungling King?
Come to his aid alone and patch his blunders,
Tied to the hot Archbishop and cold Church?
Enter the crumbling warrens of the Court,
Phosphorescent in decay, and tainted Council,
With Arundel and Holland, Henry Vane
And all 'the Queen's men' itching for his ruin?

Yet never had he done so much, so quickly:
Ireland and back again, his mind on fire
To force his failing body—there and back,
Armed with four subsidies and public vows.
And ill already, to the captain's terror
Puts out from Howth, beats out the storm to Chester
Through twenty hours of torment, where he touches
Half-dead with pain but, carried on to London,
Hurries to Charles and grips the wavering Council:

Bears down his enemies—the Queen his convert—
Levies, advises and devises, puts to shame,
And counsels a new Parliament; it meets,
But dashed and snatched away by Vane,
Leaves him alone again.
                    And so at length
Comes a new General and unprovided,
To that 'lost business' in the North, and there
They have him in their noose, their traitors' truce—
The league with Scotland.

V

Yet in the 'strange mistaking of these times'
(He will not say, their taste for blood and lies)
Something breaks out of him, astonishing
Old friends and enemies alike, so new
It seemed in him, a gentleness, a sweetness,
Born of the wreck of fortune, 'this my night.'

Was it a confidence in innocence—
For anyone can see his innocence?
'God's hand is with us, and to my best judgement
We rather win than lose . . .'
                      And as it lingered,
'All will be well, and every hour
Brings us more hope than other.'

Or was it faith in that poor Stuart's word
That he should never die while Charles was King?

Or was it over and above,
That 'Strafford would not die a fool'?
And when that fettered angel
Of his burning, winged intelligence
Had seen the blood and malice that men love,
For all their godly rage and godly lies;
Still looking back on faith and right
He found his reasons bathed in light,
And 'being upon his life and children',
Learning patience after strife,
Wrote the absolving letter
To the King, and in all sadness
Placed in his hands the 'things most loved, most dreaded,
Death or Life.'

'Sir, my consent herein shall more acquit you
To God, than all the world can do beside';

'There is no injury done to a willing man.'
'To say, Sir, that there hath not been a strife
Within me, were to make me less than man,
God knows . . .'
                    And thinking still of Will and Nan,
'My poor son and his sisters',
He will beg for them the King's regard
'No more or less hereafter, than hereafter
Their father may seem worthy of this death.'

        VI

So ends the letter. Two days later Charles
Had signed the warrant weeping, while the mob
Cumbered the yard at Whitehall.
Judges and Bishops barrenly opined:
'As it was put to us, the case was treason';
'Kings have two consciences, the public cloaks you here.'
Juxon alone said 'Follow your own conscience.'
So this earl ended.

                    And the lasting moral?
Something on geese and mice, or rats and lions?
An eagle torn by jackals?
                            'Strafford's innocent blood
Taught Charles to die'?
                            For after seven years,
He reckoned it the purchase of his death:
'An unjust sentence
That I suffered once to pass me by,
Brings me an unjust sentence.'

VII

But turning to the great man from the small,
Should we not think of Strafford after all
As of the kind
Who 'pilgrim it out here'
Some years, and 'tug and tow',
But labour, drudge unconsciously, to find
Their way to self-destruction?
And further, in the way assigned,
As one who tasted justice by injustice, murdered here,
His thirst for justice quenched when all is clear,
And he is right and they are wrong and he can say
'They have my body, but my soul is God's',
Remembering the words of Jacques Molay.

—The silver river ruffled in the breeze,
Running by grey mud-banks; the glimmering hill-circle
Closes, and opens wider . . .
      And at dawn,
And coming from the Tower he sees
The sun lift up his head, and lifting up his head,
He goes forth 'like a general breathing victory,
That leads a loving army',
But with no army to be led,
And walks between the people thick as trees.
Mounting the scaffold, granted time for speech—
Delivered standing on the hollow wood,
And turning words and gestures to the multitude;
Unheard by most and yet, it may be, not misunderstood:
As first, he thinks it strange a people should
'Choose to begin their happiness in blood';
Submits to death as voted for their good, the common good,
But not as just: 'Here we misjudge each other;
Righteous judgement, that shall come hereafter.'

And so he ends 'forgiving all the world
From my dislodging soul.'
                              Then kisses Ussher and his brother,
Unbuttons at the neck, puts up his hair,
Forgives the axe his coming stroke,
And having knelt awhile in prayer
—The head falls from the block,
Caught up and held, the people shout approof
And shake the air.
One touch of azure breaks the cloudy crumbling roof
Hung far above the tumult,
And the piece of paper whence he read
Flutters and drops, unheeded
For the trophy of the bleeding head;
But gathered up by Rushworth,
Creased, and speckled with a faded red
Comes to be published after fifty years
—When most who could remember would be dead,

Or only wished that Strafford were forgotten.

Autumn Journey

I saw from the gliding train
A yellow birch in the woods below,
And the dark pines close in again,
And thought of dry leaves falling slow
Under the cold cloud-shadows,
Horses of shadow, loosed in dreams;
And of the Snow Queen, pale and fair,
And Gerda looking for her Kay,
Poor Gerda, when she met the crow
Who led her in by the back way.
So, as they climbed the castle stair
To reach the bedroom where he lay,
Dark horses plunged like shadows,
Long-legged on the wall, in dreams;
And Gerda, while her heart beat fast,
Came where he slept, half turned away,
And called him, and the dreams rushed past,
And he awoke, and was not Kay.

Sea View

Sunlight catches a wall,
It glows, and I recall
Ten years ago our walk,
And how we sat to stare,
Quite happy not to talk,
Blown by the mild sea-air:
The bench in wind and sun
Above the pearl-grey sea,
Perched on the broken cliff,
The joy, the strange fragility—
Precarious, conscious, pleased—
The youth in everything,
Sweet, and yet not appeased
By all our love could bring.

And then the sunny quay,
The ferry churning clear,
Gulls idling on the sea,
And there along the pier
The little trundling train!
No doubt it trundles on,
As I do, but again
Grown sad that you are gone.

Handfast Point

Pale cliffs and sky
Grow dim, and dimmer;
The headlands die,
And scarcely glimmer.
Night climbs, and in a breeze
Touches the trees.

The house is still,
And the grey moths flit
Under the hill
That covers it;
And catching the sea's hiss,
We dream, not kiss.

And one star glows
In the peach-pale west,
And nothing shows
On the bay's dark breast,
And ghostly whispers pass
Through the dry grass.

At Beaulieu

Tall oaks are
Speckled yellow
At the edges,
By that grey wreck
De Bello
Loco Regis.

And there on view
Is what they
Call a heart-
coffin for two:
Crumbled away
In part,

Two cells or
Cavities
In a stone block,
Are as for
Heart's ease
Cut to interlock;

And still insconce
One green-
glazed broken cup,
Where a heart once
Had been
Closed and laid up.

Memoirs in Oxford

Memoirs in Oxford

I

The sun shines on the gliding river,
   The river shines and presses through
Damp meadows and just yellowing trees;
The tall trees left without a breeze
   Stand up against the blue.

And on one side a space for cows is
   Fenced off with willow stumps and wires;
While there the place of learning drowses,
Churches and colleges and houses
   Lifting their domes and towers and spires.

I can remember coming here
   For the first time, and in the sun
Of such an autumn, gold and clear.
I walked alone; it was the year
   Of 'crisis', nineteen thirty-one.

Frenchmen were wearing in lapels
   Ne me parlez pas de la crise!
And one could feel the chill on stricken
England, the twilight that would thicken
   And storm-wind waiting for the trees.

    *

We see that time as a beginning
   Now; but that only made it worse
For those beginning absolutely—
The sense of everything acutely
   Set going in reverse.

Young men spend too much time on time,
　Trading in futures; jostling, shoving,
They strain their gullets and digestions
With gnat-like and camelious questions,
　Designs for living, looting, loving.

That airy Stock Exchange would rock—
　Be less like fancying shirts and ties.
Hitler's 'eleventh hour' came duly—
Pits, ogres; but my own were truly
　Of quite another shape and size.

And here am I now forced to try,
　Thirty years later as it is,
To take their measure and unravel
Before and after—look and travel
　Back over opportunities

I missed! And can I now forgive
　Myself for having missed so much?
I was afraid to take or give,
Disabled or unfit to live
　And love—reach out and touch.

　　　*

It hangs in sunlight now past change
　And what is worse, beyond disguise.
That past I meet is looking strange,
But says we must be friends, arrange
　The meeting—and allow no lies.

Old faded photographs can so
　Look new to us, and I have one
Here of my mother, I can show.
I took it all those years ago
　And here, in the December sun.

Dressed warmly, with her sense and touch
   Of rightness, by the elm-tree bole
She stands; too calm to be called tense,
Yet some defiance or defence
   Looks out of her from top to sole.

It must have been my second year.
   One sees the pang that all along
She had suppressed—and more was here,
More on the way: she looks quite clear
   On that; and she would not be wrong.

Not that I grant her prophecy
   Of even how the world would go.
And some bad cards for her and me
The pack held, that she could not see—
   Some she would never know.

But she might ask what miscreated
   A nature ardent and direct
In childhood, leaving it self-hated,
Self-punishing: and what awaited
   The boy she could not now protect?

I could not tell but had to live
   The change, and suffer—cold, confined,
Withholding what I had to give,
The love I craved; a sensitive
   Of the most complicated kind.

       *

Cut off from old simplicities
   Others had carefully been taught
And could observe in their unease;
Among my other nudities
   I had but my bare-footed thought.

A precious urchin of the mind,
    It was my theory I migrated
To meet with some of my own kind:
Prig—dandy—*bel esprit*? to find
    The whole scenario was dated.

Old Mole was burrowing far and wide.
    Dangers and deaths I had not reckoned
(Much like the gulf that went beside
Pascal) appeared and multiplied;
    And I stood still whatever beckoned.

                    *

The others were a race of gods!
    Over the gap of our disjunction
I scanned their features, mouth and eyes,
Wondering if there could lie the prize;
    But had no foothold, root or function.

Yet it was odd, nor man nor God
    (Who had apparently put a curse on
My youth, and I must pay for it)
Could bring me simply to admit
    I might be an impossible person.

But that perhaps was grounded in
    My sense of being right and good—
A stubborn sense quite feminine
Or childish, of the love within,
    And wanting only what I should.

Therefore I would go on in pain
    And still come back however often
Disappointed; tug the chain
That cut the heart, and try again
    Rather than be appeased or soften.

All I had left was the conviction
    Everything should be different far;
But how? Perhaps I understood
It would be different when it could.
    Meanwhile there was a bar.

*

Well, so the enterprise takes off
    From that sad queasy unattractive
Middle-aged hindsight, in its trough
Of vain regrets—at which we scoff?
    Yes, but if one can make it active,

What may come out of it can never
    Be less than evidence—agree
With this or that view, prove whatever
You like; my safety and endeavour
    Are but to give you what I see.

So like a hermit with a flask
    Of ink I sit and drive a quill;
Push on, bent over at the task
Of truth-telling. And if I ask
    Why, it is at a demon's will.

Some god or demon turns a pin;
    A door swings open, cut in rock.
The door shuts, and I am shut in
With pen and paper, to begin
    My calculations and unlock

Old passages and messages,
    And wrestle till they come out right.
Only if then there seems to fall
Sometimes on the rocky wall,
    Melting it, a patch of light,

Quivering, shifting, soft and bright—
    It is an angel of the Lord!
For it brings the hope of flight,
With the sense of what I write
    Living of its own accord.

II

Somewhere in Mauriac a girl
   Sees the young man (the so-recurring
Young man in Mauriac) as 'preserved',
That is to say untouched, reserved;
   And wonders to herself, demurring,

'For what?...' All things are preparations:
   Our birth and parentage—when, where—
And the ups and downs of foreign nations;
Sunsets and pets and railway-stations;
   The nursery frieze, an old Scotch air.

And English and French novelists
   Once dwelt on home as preparation
Through good plain love. If asked 'For what?'
They might have said at least 'Why not
   To live again in our narration?'

     *

It was a wide blue British sky
   That arched above deep seas in foam,
Where ships in glossy paint went by
To India, China and Shanghai,
   And back to England, back to 'home'.

And liners and hotels had *Punch*
   And *Ideal Homes*, the *Tatler*, *Sphere*
And the *Illustrated London News;*
Cartoons by H. M. Bateman; views
   From the Matopos to Kashmir.

That world was ours, no matter where;
    So brave and staid it stretched away
Through the unthinking pastimes of
Colonial England, bridge and golf,
    Tea-parties—tea four times a day—

Saturday racing, drives on Sunday . . .
    Yet through those acres of dry thorn
And sun and dust and boulders ran—
Not quite a ghost—a thought of man
    And God and law; not quite outworn.

Trophies and scars of faded wars,
    A hillside grave seen from the train;
An empty blockhouse by the bridge
And granite needle on the ridge,
    Might tell of greed and pride and pain.

And the other, further war (of course
    We won) was worse—incomprehensible!
But reason surely must increase
And what was left of hatred cease;
    That would be only sensible.

            *

My father from the time I claim
    Remembrance, on his mantel-shelf
Had standing always in the same
Silver and dark-blue velvet frame
    A small old photograph of himself:

At twenty, at his most beautiful—
    Long-jacketed, pale-faced, dark-eyed.
Like a young moon that nears the full
And gazes on a twilight pool,
    His head was tilted to one side.

I had left home before he died,
    Young as the picture showed him then.
Afterwards—sore, unsatisfied,
I begged it and was not denied;
    But it had gone, no one knew when

Or where! And I recall the room,
    The silence. No one spoke because
Everyone saw the question loom
'He had given it—but to whom?'
    We held our breath and left the pause.

*

My mother blamed his education
    For faults and lessons never learned:
His puns and self-depreciation,
Wrong choice of friends, and speculation—
    Gambling with money so well-earned.

Thinking himself a common man
    He gave himself with too much trust.
Stubborn in weakness, dumb in pride—
His deepest hopes unsatisfied
    Were apt to end in self-disgust.

I had adored then hatefully
    Rejected him, in an immense
Hard rage and boyish misery.
Yet now in all he was I see
    A strange and saving innocence.

I grieve that we were never friends.
    It hurts; but neither would know how.
What that I say can make amends?
I leave it, knowing how it ends,
    And love him as I see him now.

For now he is beyond our reach
    I share and understand too well—
And let his love of music teach
Me, like a touch not needing speech—
    Things he could never tell.

      *

But I must thank my mother's mind,
    Her fiery rational sense of right
And love of all things well-designed,
Books, furniture and people—signed
    With logic, courage, wit and light.

She gave us pictures and adventures,
    Ballads and stories by the fire,
Echoes of Ruskin and Carlyle,
The notion that there could be 'style';
    But most herself and her desire.

She *was* Jane Eyre and Maggie Tulliver,
    Those ardent women! only free,
After such hardships—childhood scrapes,
Young visions, efforts and escapes—
    As in the mind's eye we could see.

And we were Oliver and Jim
    Hawkins and David Copperfield;
And Absalom with gold hair in
The Bible, and young Benjamin
    And Jairus' daughter that was healed.

I owe her my delight in verse
    But some part too of misery—
Were that for better or for worse:
Fear of 'the body' like a curse,
    That so long would bewilder me.

      *

She had wished that she could believe;
    Said once 'the basis of our lives
Is wrong'; and once that she could feel
Something mysterious, an appeal
    That 'opens like a flower—revives'.

For he died early, she lived on,
    Through all the latter part of life
Bitter, but gradually less,
And chafing yet not comfortless.
    But now, the thought is like a knife,

That they could have such confidence
    And win so far, but be defeated!
Nothing be left of it at length,
Their hope, young arrogance and strength—
    Their work undone or uncompleted.

But—childhood, music in the summer
    Garden and the first fire lit
On a cold sunny afternoon;
Apricot blossom—bees in tune—
    Butterflies that alight and sit

And sun themselves and wag their wings!...
    Our moderate greatness went awry,
But not before we had these things,
Fenced with their love; and if it wrings
    The memory, that all went by—

Yet they were lucky all the same,
    Both he and she, and those who live
Have far more to regret or blame.
We only took, but they can claim
    They taught the way to give.

III

Fretted discoloured towers and domes
   And crumbling walls that rose upright:
Their mixture of the dry and rich
And dull, made up a message which
   At times looked heavy—void of light.

And many times the buildings lay
   With a dead weight like paving-stones
On my sick heart. What did they say,
Law—duty—God? It seemed a way
   Of death in life, like skull and bones;

So old, sardonically old!
   And they looked so much older then;
Not as they do, re-faced and bold
And looking down in grey and gold
   On other, younger men.

While my young face has left me, if
   It leaves me with a mind unfaded—
Indeed less faded; for my thought
Was styptic, withering what it brought,
   And self-despised and self-invaded.

So old, so battered, so forlorn
   I might have seemed at twenty-one;
A breathing body yet unborn,
Or blown, and withering on the thorn—
   Ten poor enigmas tied in one.

*

Things that look small at such a space
  Can yet be bitter on the tongue.
But is that all—a common case,
Where we can smile and say this place
  Like youth, is wasted on the young?

I take it further. Sitting at
  My table, if I care to look
I see a little grassy plat
Hidden behind the college, that
  Contrives a garden in the nook.

A green bronze athlete lifts his hand,
  Head bent beneath the clustered towers.
The airy path is wide and free
That leads to wounds and agony—
  Death, glory—in this war of ours.

There I launched out, and if I see
  Returning it is no less true
That I was wretched here, I find
The wretchedness itself a kind
  Of gage, a promise, a way through,

A way of beating out my fate:
  To seize and carry early on
The nameless difference like a weight;
What I would be in love and hate—
  Etiam si omnes ego non.

                    *

Put the case, and I see myself
  Quite easily as other than
I am—a question-mark below it;
Not mad enough to be a poet
  But a successful active man,

Architect, engineer or lawyer.
    How can one think the self away
Or feel identity can change?
Yet occupations to estrange
    Me less, might well have come my way.

But above others hard to seek
    Instead—of all most difficult
The kingdom that I chose was weak,
Neglected, poor; the way oblique
    And quite uncertain of result.

—It was no choice, I could not choose.
    Much rather had it caught me, pinned
Or pinioned by a leash, a bond
Of cobweb, to a thought beyond
    This earth and sea and sun and wind;

Dying and burning in faint fire
    As if spring feared to come and trod
Half-cowering, shivering in desire
And naked in that thin attire
    Of bud and twig and dusty clod.

For so I figure it, as weak,
    Uncertain; but a thing 'of might',
A thread that leads to the abyss
Of love, thought, death. And it was this
    That held me, drew to harder sight:

Held me half-blinded by my need
    Or by slow torment drew me on;
Forced me to know myself and heed
My own necessities indeed.
    Yet when I summoned it, was gone.

*

And time would pass and here there was
    Nothing, for me no end in view.
Ranging I thought it might appear,
Though sure of nothing but a fear
    Of finding nothing new.

So I remember other places—
    Mountains and tenements and towns;
Shadows of trees in lighted squares;
Cafés, the sound of distant fairs,
    And woods and fields and downs.

I saw new faces, rare pure faces
    Or hard and coarse, but as before
Was held back even by the intense
Perception—like a violence
    That crouched and would recoil in war.

Drawn out, drawn forward by the sight,
    Not dead at heart but separated—
Separated by that 'weak might',
The lack of meaning, from delight.
    —Slowly the elements related:

The endless aching waste of feeling
    And death, some kind of purity;
That silent madness of my youth,
The need—and hope and fear—of truth
    Must be the same as poetry.

Yes, and must be the same as faith!
    The mind might shudder and misgive,
But that weak power would pine and grieve,
And press the thought that to believe
    Would be—it must—the way to live.

A light broke in the thought that love
   Can earn love: as it crossed my brain
'Surely this longing must draw love.'
I can remember it, above
   A patch of woodland, in a lane.

There were some voices in the distance,
   Children at play. It was a dull
Day, but one felt the spring for sure,
The faint warm breath; and then that pure
   Insight that nothing could annul.

*

I have my clue that takes me through
   And as it led me glimmering there,
Brings me to an imperfect saint,
Longing for certainty and faint
   From the uncertainties of prayer.

Sant'Angela who was perhaps
   No more a saint than me or you,
Escaped the canon; and one sees
Why—there is sorrow and unease
   In all she does or tries to do.

—Sorrow, unease or desperation:
   But that is why she offers me
An emblem of the hope and strife
And death in life—the choice of life
   In death—I'd have you see.

*

She tells how passing by the church
   Alone in the deserted square
She could hardly walk or stand;
An impulse gripped her like a hand,
   To throw herself down in despair.

She would imagine some wild death
   High in the mountains, by a shrine
With broken boulders. Or a word
Seemed spoken, that she thought absurd:
   'I have chosen you, you are mine.'

She would resist and mock, deny it,
   Until one day she chanced to see
The picture of a saint embraced
By Christ, with arms about his waist;
   And it said 'So you could be.'

The picture must have been of Francis.
   And still it said to her 'So you
Could be'; and she would put it by—
Laugh at it secretly and try
   To prove it never could be true.

What shall we say of weirder fancies—
   Her taste for bitter food, and sighing
To have a death accompanied
With ridicule and shame; her need
   To be near the sick and dying?

She asked God why he made man—why,
   Once having made him, let him sin?
And why redeem the world by pain?
Then it would suddenly be plain,
   As if daylight entered in:

That God could have done otherwise
   But nothing better, she could see.
And then she saw beyond her will
A thing fixed and unshakeable
   And calm, like a decree;

Which she could only say was all-good.
　　She saw no love, but this fixed thing;
And in the wafer of the bread
A fair boy sitting, crown on head,
　　With a gold rod and a ring.

Therefore she had felt certainty,
　　Saw with the eyes of faith and peace
The evidence—looked piercingly,
Intently, into clarity;
　　So that she thought it could not cease.

Yet she had watched it out of sight,
　　And again saw herself dejected!
Naked, in wretchedness of mind
And choked with faults of every kind;
　　If chosen, chosen to be rejected.

　　　　＊

She left no teaching or advice,
　　Only what she had seen and known—
Plain statements if the soul can read:
Too bitter and too hard to plead
　　For any failure but her own;

But look at them as thought, as need,
　　Hunger—it is alive, a version
Of living out the dream, by light
And darkness, through mistrust and fright;
　　But most through silence and desertion.

IV

Plato says that in Heaven there is
    Laid up the pattern of a city
Which the man who desires it sees;
And he can follow its decrees
    And live in justice, truth and pity.

Whether it does or ever will
    Exist, that city, is another
Matter: the man who sees it still
Can live according to its will,
    And be subject to no other.

Nothing could on the face of it
    Be less like my experience
Than Plato's claim—that I admit.
And yet it can be made to fit
    I think, the glimpse I had, the sense

Of that 'poor kingdom'. There it stood
    Waiting, if one but stopped and groped—
Waiting for one who never came,
Or passed—the empty path, a name;
    And some were dead who loved and hoped . . .

—Or as a lamp shines on a ceiling,
    The curtains wide: through foggy night
One sees it from the country lane,
Feels quiet warm life behind the pane—
    There if one could decide aright,

There if one would!... It was the hope
    Within my hope, that gave it wings;
However it may sound obscure
The thing itself is clear and sure—
    Not the exigencies it brings.

                *

Or so I think this afternoon,
    And passing through a Roman arch
Of yellow stone vermiculated,
Sit down and ponder in belated
    Sunshine, by a tuft of larch.

The gardens are for birds in bushes
    And one slow fountain; walled in stone
And set on low ground by the river,
They shelter—though the tree-tops quiver,
    Continually, lightly blown.

So light a stir will not deter
    The bees which are intent on going
Through that wistaria on the wall.
The sprays of blossom break and fall
    And dangle, honey-scented, glowing.

And yet their delicate mauve clusters
    Even in this good year are muffled
By that peculiar silky pale
Brown foliage; they had been too frail
    To come without it, chilled and ruffled.

You must have seen a plant like this,
    In some strange climate but assuming
The task of being what it is—
Spreading and budding, not to miss
    The happiness of blooming.

Finally it is rich and sweet—
    Spills, offers up the incense hoarded
In penury; the robe it spun
Floats and is starry in the sun;
    All that was drab or sad and sordid

Melts into light! And looked at so,
    Of course the plant has come together
With life, thought, impulse—all one sees
As lasting through our century's
    Long tale of broken weather.

         *

For so we live it out displaced,
    And caught by every wind that blows:
Revolt, mere flatulence or waste—
Terror, confusion—loveless haste,
    And malice reaping as it sows.

And all these things can blast the spirit
    And leave it old, and ill, and mad.
But I survived and persevered—
Even had luck, as it appeared;
    So I was given—what I had.

And that was—well, what any man
    At times, and even the dead world knows,
And every line should have conveyed.
If not, it is too late; they fade,
    The wind drops and the sunlight goes,

And I can only moralise
    What Plato said. There was a vision—
Verse, music—but the centre lies
Beyond; and my wistaria tries,
    Lives and will die, the soul in prison,

To give itself in love and light.
    Which if we do, the rest is 'sent';
Nothing that comes can come amiss,
No evil, loss or pain. And this
    May be what Plato meant.

V

Being *incontentabile*
　　Like Foscolo, in making verse;
Not to be satisfied but lingering
Cutting, cancelling, rubbing, fingering—
　　And sometimes changing bad for worse;

I might do better to end here,
　　Put down the pen and close my eyes.
But only to be free I'll add
One other memory I had,
　　That nothing else will exorcise.

I'll call up Shelley, give him thanks
　　And praise, tell him in gratitude
How at about thirteen I won
Some books at school—his book was one—
　　And how it rapt my solitude.

That book begot a dream in me—
　　To wander out alone and bare
And be a naked man and free
(And yet one would not want to be
　　Alone, another should be there . . .)

But opening to the wilderness
　　Of light, air, music, in the sun
Be fused with all and not repress
Love, joy and goodness that could bless
　　The universe and make it one;

Be drunk with dew and winds that blow
    Sand-dunes and budding thorns, and hope—
A sweetness like the form and glow
Of human limbs—the body so
    Alive and quivering, to have scope!

*

You lie nearby, carved as if found
    Washed up in nakedness, dead-white
And lax; yet not released but bound
In marble, and more deeply drowned
    By that almost subaqueous light.

So at last broken, there you lie.
    —No, but you breathe and burn and shine,
And from the breaking wave and dying
Flame, and the withered leaf and flying
    Cloud on the barren Apennine,

The rays go out, grow out, shine here—
    Everywhere! And who knows what share
You had in this, my coming here
And my desire and hope and fear;
    And all that came of it elsewhere?

*

It is all like a damp-stained book,
    England, an old biography—
Layer on layer where we look
Dismayed at what those people took
    For life, supposing it to be

Their melancholy public labours!
    —Not Shelley's verse that spurns the crowd,
Breaks from the wreck of empires, wars,
Rebellions, and flings wide the doors
    To dappled moonlight, burning cloud . . .

I catch at visions, worlds in brief
    That point to the unchangeable,
As if I could insert a leaf
Illumined in the same belief
    In art and thought and living will.

It would be like a hymn, a creed;
    Yet I began with no such aim,
But looked for meaning in the past,
Youth and frustration, and at last
    This was the way it came.

Drypoints of the Hasidim

'Why are the people dancing?' ask the deaf ones,
'Why are they running after the musicians?'

Drypoints of the Hasidim

I

Dark hollow faces under caps
In days and lands of exile

And among unlettered tribes
                              eternal names

Like Aryeh, Elimelech, Aaron, Zusya
    And Yerahmiel
                    yoked now by chance to places
Otherwise unremarkable like Apt
    Or Medzibosh or Zans

                              And pedlars, tailors
Weavers of woollen stockings, metal-workers
    Dispersed in hamlets of the Pale
Or in Podolia and Volhynia
                        keeping inns

Tanners and cobblers, pharmacists, horse-doctors
Corn-factors or arendars to a Polish lord
                        (distilling
    And milling for him) or confined to trade
In wax and furs and clothing and horned cattle

—Dark, ruddy white or sallow fair!
And some with sun-dried cheeks and hair,
    Rough, wearing sheepskin

Riding and plodding on bad roads
By valleys in the dark Carpathians
                        threaded with tawny crystal

Past battered cottages and farms
With yellow middens and a dog in chains,
    And osiers by a stream

        2

Hundreds and thousands died
                    or hundred thousands

Had died, and they would go on dying
    In those contested lands and yet live on;

Increase in cabined wooden houses
    Leaning together for support,
In back-streets or on the outskirts
    Of shabby towns like Okop
Or Mogilev or Minsk

                Think of the signs
In towns like Okop, Mogilev and Minsk:
                    The house of prayer,
Schoolhouse and bath
                and in each family
A few worn candlesticks, books, cups and linen;
    A table scrubbed
                the humble
Apparatus of prayer

                Thin boys in *yeshivahs*
At twilight with an oil lamp
    And the first light fall of snow
Feathering the window-panes;
    A stove and chest of books,
Abseys in Hebrew
                where they can whet the edges
Of little eagle wits and eyes
                —Poor Talmudists
Glad to be kept as ushers, hoping to be elect

(There might be years of study,
Poverty, near starvation,
   Perhaps with a young wife and child
Living at home with parents)

                        Pipe-smoking rabbis
Learning the hatred of the world!
   Teaching and festivals and prayer,
And dancing in the summer evening
   Fiddlers and wine-cups at the inn;

   And moonlight silvering wooden walls
And greasy alleys and the market square
   Left empty but for litter

      3
Dov Baer the Maggid of Mesritch
Would argue that true thoughts and purposes
   And meanings
                  can shine out only in ends:

'Thus when men saw God manifest his glory
In Egypt
         and the miracle of the Red Sea
   They could not know what end he had in view;
But later
         when he gave the Law on Sinai
   They could see it was that Israel
Might wear it as a crown

                  'Likewise' he said
'I see created worlds and things,
   But not their use or purpose
                        until I see
The people of Israel, when I know at once

'They are the purpose of the world'

4

Well, but if so,
What of that sign of contradiction
  The condition of the Jews
                   the wandering Shekhinah,
The beauty-who-has-lost-her-eyes?

  And what if underneath it all
There is a taste of injury, a bitterness
  A grudge, a sense of being born
To suffer and be weary
                 living in separation
And the necessity of being bad?

                'From birth to death'
  (The voices of the old men saying)
'We have been like a pent-up sluice, our lives
  A desecrated service;
Here we have no place to rejoice'

             Or else accusing God
Like the tailor at Yom Kippur who said
                'God,
  You had better forgive me:

'I might have kept back a few pieces of cloth
  Or eaten without washing my hands
In some non-Jewish house where I was working;

'But you have taken away the mother from her child,
  Children from mothers

'And you have scattered us across the world'

II

I

To believe is above all to be in love,
And suffer as men do who are in love.

   The story has it that one day
One Friday, when the zaddik makes
   His self-examination
                  a disciple found the Besht
So emptied of himself and crushed, in darkness
   And dereliction
            the last breath
Of life had almost left him;

   And was so terrified all he could say
Was
     'My master and my teacher . . .'

   But those words were enough
To reach his heart and bring it back from death

2

There you have everything
                          that name
A kind of joy surrounding it,
  The Baal Shem Tov:

The Master of the Good Name,
  A healer in the name of God

A poor man and not learned;
  But he could overcome division
Between clean and unclean
                    the holy sparks
  And evil urge within a man

'The process lies in giving shape
To formless forces, dragons, *kelipoth* . . .'

And he could shake the worlds in prayer
                    that could be seen
When wheat-grains trembled, trembled in an open sack
  And water in a jug

And he could offer them the prize
  Of heart-prayer, with the sudden burst of light—
Fire light honey light—
  And silent music and invisible eyes

That shut the eyes of the mind and yet give sight

3

With that they have new thoughts of good and evil,
   And evil as cast or withered good
                              that come
After the deep wound dealt by that deceiver
   Sabbatai Zevi

               —Who also had belonged
Like all such prophets and themselves
                    to 'the last times'
Of impiety and confusion,
   And had brought about the fall
Of many in Israel whom he told to sin
   Freely because the last times were at hand.

                    Yet so it was
   That after he had damned himself and them,
Israel ben Eliezer the Baal Shem
   Could say
          'In evil also we find good':

'Torah the seed of justice
   Like the sun giving light
Builds upon evil
               and the powers of evil
   Are but a throne for good'

   He also said
            'The man who sins
Burns the whole Torah in the eyes of God.
   But we should say
               It is enough for me

'*If he has this or that good quality*'

4

For if the holy sparks in things
Are separated from God, so are the Jews.

Everything is in exile
                    everything will return
Because everything desires to be redeemed—
    Everything in the world and worldliness—

Not to be emptied of itself or worldliness
But to be hallowed in the *kawannoth*

                              And Israel
Seeming helpless in dispersal
                    soiled
    And failing of the Law and prayer
Can be that suffering consciousness

And bid for the return of all
                    the 'turning'

(And Bunam in that stinking room
At Danzig, where he had turned in to pray
    Went pale and shrank and turned away

But turned back, for he said
                    'The very walls

'Would arraign God, if I rejected them')

III

1

But they are telling stories,
   Stories of kings and sons of kings

Of hidden just men who could be Messiahs
   Had they not put away the thought;
Rays, glimpses in shadow
                and that sweetness—
   Love justice sonship brotherhood—
Which makes the longing of the world:

                Messiah son of Joseph,
Who could be anywhere
            a youth half-grown
   Born anywhere in Hungary or Poland

   —Perhaps the boy of seventeen
Who had undoubtedly been seen
   In Buda, with a threadbare coat

And face of an amazing starlike purity

2

And debts and wagers, prophecies and wonders!
   Witty constructions on a famous crux,
Jokes and ingenious repartees and guesses

   And how one said of some deep thought
Much like a dictum of his own
   But cited as another man's
              'He had it

From the Babylonian Talmud
                              but I had it—

'From where the Talmud had it'

         3
    And so they tell and tell again
This or that well-known story

                              Of the zaddik
Alone in birch-woods in the summer evening,
    Or at the third meal on the Sabbath
(The Sabbath like a rope let down
    One day a week from Heaven)

    —Jacob Joseph of Polnoye
They tell us, had a very restless face

    Yisakhar Baer or Berel as a young man
Was so poor he had not eaten for some days:

    'Now in those days the bath at Radoshitz
Was sixty or seventy steps below ground level;
    Yisakhar Baer undressed down to his shirt
And took a light and started on his way . . .'

—Follows a tale of evil powers
    Calling through darkness, clapping hands on water
Brushing his cheeks with dirty wings,
    But baffled in the end

And other stories of strange powers:
    Drives in the country, villages at dawn

Dull pools in early light
                And how
The Baal Shem driving with some friends at night
   Dozed off, and suddenly a wood sprang up
And blocked the road

               They woke him and the wood
  Drew back in darkness, but a voice

Said softly, gruffly
            'You should take more care'

    4
  And Moshe of Sambor, Zevi Hirsh's brother
As a boy went trading in the villages

  And once he asked his brother and his teacher
Why, when he came back at the end of day
  For the Afternoon Prayer
              and began to pray
He felt a glory flooding his whole body?

  And Zevi Hirsh had said
           'Why be surprised?

'When a traveller walks in the ways of God
  Through fields and by-ways
           whether he knows or not,
The divine sparks in the trees and plants and stones
  Are drawn forth to attach themselves and shine in him;

  'And Isaac, it is written
Went out in the field to meditate at evening'

5

And the Yehudi told a visitor at Parsischa,
   Kalman of Cracow
               that he had
Among his pupils one in whose face could be seen
   The full image of God

   And Kalman went round with a light
Shielding it with his hand,
   When the disciples were asleep
Looking at each in turn, holding his breath:

Until he found behind the stove
   (Faint stir of embers in the stove)
The young man Shelomo Leib.
               And Kalman looking,

Half-nodding had agreed
          'Yes, it is true'

6

Blessing the new moon in the month he died
   The Rabbi of Berditchev had preached at supper
On the upright man and death.
             Then he said grace
   And walked about the room

             And his face glowed,
And he stood beside the table and said
          'Good table,

   'You are and can be witness
I have eaten and taught rightly at your board:

'So I shall have you made into my coffin'

7

Hayyim of Zans who liked to talk
To market-people, would tell of one who said:

'Good sir, I have got nothing out of life.
   I spend my time day after day
Jogging and shuttling to and fro from Hanipol
   To Brod
         and climbing in and out of carts,
And being thought a cheat;
   But what is this when one considers

'How beyond boredom and disgust, how sweet it is
   To be able to know and say
I can enter any night or day
             myself
   In my nakedness before the Holy One:

'To bathe in God, to pray'

IV

1

The same grey path covered with last year's leaves.

—And the light of day shines down
                                    the world goes on
And their enemies are not now the *mitnaggedim*,
    Learned and orthodox
                        But rather 'Germans',
'So–called enlightened ones'
                            in other words

    The faithless of another generation
Who have done better for themselves
                                    and mock
At poverty and dirt among the Poles,
                        quoting from Scripture

'The wise man will not wear a spotted robe'

2

And no doubt there would always be, there must be
    Two minds, two dispositions
                            Like the two friends
Boys, dear companions
                    one of whom will say
    'It is so'
            and the other 'No, not so'

But the real ending is not like that story,
Which is of love and faith come back from death

    For there are others,

Others who will come close and say
    Like some from Lubavitch
                'I have a secret'

And the secret is there is no secret
                      nothing;
    No true belief, no ecstasy, no way
Nothing
        and those who know it but pretend
                   Put on a face
For reasons that are more or less unbeautiful.

    And so they travel through the ways
Of all such pious companies
                and spread,
    Spread irresistibly
            and sink, undo
What they had come to do

    As they had gone out to the people
The people had come in, eager to catch
    The crown of the anointed
                 (surging of angels
And the figures of old men, Elijah, Abraham
    And the trembling of the worlds)
                   but lost the way

Because they cannot quite believe there is a way

3

So Bunam, tired
                    half-sick of reading *kvitlach*
(So-called the little notes on slips of paper
    A zaddik would be given, for his prayers)

    Small grubby problems and petitions
So abject
                    Bunam gave his friends a parable;

    Of a king's son as usual,
Who had run away from home:

                                    'And after years
His father sent a messenger to find him
    And be reconciled and promise anything—
Anything he could think of as a gift
                                    his dearest wish

'And the man had found him dressed in rags
                                        with bare feet
Dancing among the peasants; gave his message;
    And the young man wept, and said he would be happy

'If his father were to send a pair of shoes'

4

And Menahem Mendel said
                        'I hoped to draw
    A few serious companions
                            and with them become a flame;
But I drew multitudes
    Who turned me into water'

And as a young man looking for a teacher
                            'I want' he said 'I want
A simple Jew, a plain Jew who fears God'

But the Rabbi of Lublin had replied
   'Your way is the way of melancholy. Leave it.
It has not found favour in my eyes'

                            And Mendel
Left him for Parsischa, for the Yehudi
   And then for Kotzk
                     arriving after years
Of such fame as he detested
   And worn, tormented by his fears
Fetching up in that Friday,
   That Friday night at Kotzk

When the disciples were assembled,
And he burst out on them in a rage
                       blaspheming
   Hitting at books and candelabra
                      'Idiots!
There is no judgement and no judge.
   I am no Rabbi nor a Rabbi's son!'

And after that for nearly twenty years
He never left his room or spoke
                       but now and then
   Stood at the door with loathing in his eyes

—And even as a boy he was 'Black Mendel'
And the Yehudi when a visitor inquired
   If any of his pupils was worth-while,
Considered and said
                'Mendel
Wants to be worth-while'

5

And Schneor Zalman rightly saw
The future would be better for the common man
But worse for the exceptional man;
                         That we can also see.

But the hasid is a poor Jew, not a common man
    (And has there ever been a common man?)
Only he is not as he was
                         not like the young man

Who is younger than his years, born out of due time
    And with nothing to his name
                         No place in life,
No shelter on the face of the earth;
    But naked, hidden like a god
Breathing and burning, trembling
    Aching at heart, proud and ashamed
And angry with himself
                         is cheated and rewarded
    By his secret love and pain

—Who might go fiercely to the bad,
Damage himself and others
                         smile with a bitter joy;
    But who could also be quite changed:

And now he is like the solid grown-up man
Who has learnt how to behave,
                         behave like others
    And maybe play the fool, but not the fool of God

And now he can look back at times and wonder
How he was ever such a child, absurd,
    A misery, so hopeless

V

1

Reading their story I follow and agree
  With everything that happens:

    Some for Napoleon and Prussia,
  Some for the victory of Russia,
    With prayers on either side;
  Wars, revolutions and new liberties,
    Old and new sorrows and indignities

(And ugly ones may be redeemed
                                but ugliness

    Rises, rises again)

2

And everything had changed, all the conditions
  More than a hundred years ago
                                And well before
The old world had begun to go;
  What traces would you find today

    In Stachow or Lizhensk or Tchernobil
  But cemeteries and their leaning stones
    With carvings of two hands
                                finger on thumb?

But look back further and you see
  It is the same faith, the same pain
In those brethren of the spotted robe,
  The same in us, the same in them

Dying and yet surviving
   Contending always to survive

                              Their holy men
   Crying
         'If not now, when?'
'Why does the son of Jesse yet delay?'
                              Their only way
   Through all that hating and despising
(The soldier weeping on his iron bed)

To endure and be silent,
   Reason, rejoice and pray;
Die if you must.

                  And even Israel of Rizhyn
The great-grandson of the Maggid dressed in silk,
   White silk
                  and sitting in a golden chair
Could say
         'I have heard the blowing of the horn

'But not in this-world'

Afterword on Rupert Brooke

to Elizabeth

Afterword on Rupert Brooke

I

The way in is to pause and look again, look back
    And ask what would it be without the photographs?

Bare-throated profile with the tumbled bright young hair,
    Full face with shining eyes, and the rose-leaf and gold
Granted by our complaisance to the monochrome:
    Well, thank the American that with both hands he took
And offered us 'God's vulgar lyric *Rupert Brooke*',
    The chance an Englishman with 'good taste' might have missed
And left us with no legend, or one so much the less
    It would have less of truth.

                    For it is also true,
The legend, and not to be discarded even
    If one should now re-model and re-write so much.

Picture and legend will lose nothing, rather gain
    In potency, when to the frail rustic-heroic
And sincerely unreal memorial bronze
    Moulded, say, by Alfred Gilbert, the young lanky
Nakedness of the warrior without armour
    We add the real nudity and harder truth
That do live on through death.
                  And if we are honest,
    And if we have not misunderstood already,
And if we want to understand anything now,
    We must take all there is, and see and weigh it all
If possible, like those who loved and outlived him
    And hearing he was dead would feel unbearably
The thought 'It had to be, just that'; like Henry James
    Who bowed his head and wept and said 'Of course, of course'.

There it is then, the first thing—being beautiful
    As with a woman's beauty, and yet masculine.

There it is first and last, both *Ave* and *Vale*
    And no less inescapable because his friends
Were not pleased and demurred when others used the word,
    And tried like Frances Cornford for alternatives,
Hoping to find some quality of heart or mind
    That fitted like a key.
                            'A generosity'
She called it, 'the real reason' why his charm of face
    So took one, why it was 'continual pleasure
To look at him each day, his radiant fairness,
    Beauty of build, broad head and forehead with the hair
Flung back, the deep-set candid eyes, their steadiness
    And clearness so entirely giving him . . .'

                                            But giving,
Giving also as she could see, with the unique
    Good luck of a physique to match his character,
'A symbol of youth for all time': the disservice
    Of her poor phrase but rendering, for an irony,
The young live piercing question of *What is it for?*
    What to do and why do it?

                            Without a word, yet
It was the question he took about, like breathing.

II

The young question of *What is it for* stays always
  Young, but will be defined of course by time and place,
And in his case by the England of King Edward
  The Peacemaker, of Imperial afternoon
And Liberal noonday.
                          'Who will inherit England?'
  The novelists and Shaw and Wells debated it,
And drafted symbols of a new faith or unfaith.

But the transparency in him, identity
Of mould and moral substance made it personal,
  The question of what and why—articulated
By chance and circumstance peculiar to him
  No doubt, like being a poet and having no money—

But deeply, darkly personal with a danger
  That is written in the lucid eyes and tinge of dawn
Riding the rosy horses: a vertigo, a dread
  Thrust on him by the burden of insistent beauty
And sharpened by the failure of inbred belief
  To nausea and madness—a dread that body
And mind are one, and all youth seems and dreams is trapped by
  The seen and unseen processes of appetite,
Birth, growth, decay, and death and dirt in all of them.

So we have the uglies of his verse, like *Jealousy*,
Old Age and *Lust*, when he sees flesh go stale and sour,
  Dry, greasy and baggy, and fastens his disgust
On some young rival who prospers but will repel
  ('For he'll be dirty, dirty') in his middle age

Long-married to the girl: which brings the bitter cry
    'And you'll be dirty too!'—but also the unsaid
Angry 'And so will I'.

                Not all his 'honesty',
    And ingenuous daring and laughing wit elsewhere,
Can hide the crudity of fear and misery here,
    Or its correlative in the unreal passion
That postures in *Dust* and *Mummia*—insanely cries
    'Helen's the lips I press' 'I tangle Egypt's hair'
'Two Antonies are mirrored in your eyes!' and fancies
    His dead lover and himself as drifting particles
Haunting the sunset air with rapture, to instruct
    A later passionless deluded pair ('Poor fools')
Who might think otherwise they knew what love could be.

    No wonder in *Dead Men's Love* the 'damned successful poet'
Would feel the wind blow cold and 'with a sick surprise
    The emptiness of eyes'.

                Feeling nothing and afraid
Of meaning nothing, he snatches roughly, fiercely
    At passion or bitterness.
                The soft bright surface
Will shudder with a fear of being 'second-rate',
    Which is not far from a fear of growing older.

III

'You go by bushes with dog-roses, through long grass,
  Harebell and scabious in the wet cow-pasture,
And through it and beyond it all feel something, some-
  thing not personal but a unity, a wholeness . . .'

But with so many clever people (too many,
  Clever or not?) all young together, all talking
And all 'advanced'?
                    Camping and walking over downs
  Or the New Forest patchwork of pine, oak and heather;
Coming back year by year to Fordingbridge and Bank
  And Bucklers Hard; looking out over Channel seas
From Dorset clifftops in the sweetness of wind-blown
  Blue weather!
                    Young people took to life out-of-doors
Then, with an impulse like his own to strip and swim
  Leaping and plunging in clear water, imaging
Their war on dingy old superstitions, trappings
  And trammels.

                    And one year as an experiment
His mother would have batches of his friends to stay
  In Somerset—some men, and Daphne, Brynhild, Gwen
Ka, Margery . . .
                    But Bryn quite blatantly prefers
  Walking alone on Exmoor to the drawing-room
With the Ranee, and she finds all the girls so odd
  In dress and conversation, and after Maynard
Keynes says evasively that she has never met
  So many brilliant and conceited young men.

                                        Sad
That his 'inexplicable sparkling people' had

So failed to please, her son made rueful fun of it;
But remained sure his lot were right in their new-found-
     out certainties and uncertainties, and to wear
Lightly or cast off the dead hand of 'those grotesque
     Encumbrances called parents'—right to undermine
Their obtuse and shabby world.

                              And if Beatrice Webb
     At her Summer School in Wales thought they were shallow,
Those Cambridge Fabians, and quite unteachable,
     And Rupert one of the worst, one can well believe
She disapproved of just what gives it colour now—
     Their politics flushed with the young easy romance
And fun, and the emblem their camping and campaigning.

     Clearly it was Rupert's emblem, when with Dudley Ward
And Dalton he went lecturing in village halls
     On the Poor Law and the Minority Report,
Or gave out Fabian pamphlets from a caravan
     In Hampshire, calling on Edward Thomas at Steep:

But also arranging that, secretly, to be
     Near Bedales and able to meet Noel Olivier.

IV

We cannot disinter the girls of nineteen-eight
    Or nine, ten and eleven, from the faded layers
Of verse, dead leaf on leaf; but Noel was last and chief,
    And gleams out impassively as in the glimpses
Which were all he had that year.

                        What she then gave him
    Was a long bitterness that grew to find her kept
So out of reach.
            (As later she would keep herself
    With Rupert's letters, and I think that fortunate:
It lives without her—with her there would have been far,
    Far too much . . .)

                    There was after all fatality
In the camp-circle of friends and his shining unease.

They say that Noel had clear hard grey eyes that looked
As if she thought him visionary and absurd,
    But would be tolerant of that extravagance.
What could be less like Ka Cox offering her kind
    Plain vulnerable face and slow 'instinctive' mind—
Or no mind, as one might in the end conjecture?

He had come closer to her lately, closer, both
To talk of wanting Noel and yes, drawn by her too.
    For Ka had always been deep in confidences,
Always ready for a 'heart-to-heart', and needed
    Always when she had lost a friend, another friend
To reassure her; and she had just lost Raverat.

So back from Munich in the summer of nineteen-
eleven, he feels a need of her at Grantchester.
    Jacques and Gwen Raverat, who are now married, have called
And left him 'drooping in front of the Old Vicarage,
    Sentimental and jealous', and most unwillingly
Alone:
            'And I have been so lofty for an hour,
So full of thoughts on Transience and Immanence
And the Larger Outlook, so—in a word, so like
    You, Ka! . . . But come, and we'll be intimate, intense
And guess, discover everything. Oh damn your aunts!
    Shall I to London?'

                        And he adds a numbered list
Of 'the best things in the world', such as Lust, weather,
    Keats, *marrons glacés*, Love and 'guts', ending with Ka
And Rupert, who can sign as Number Twenty-Nine.

    And so tempting her, teasing her and charming her,
Making her laugh, as it were singing for his supper,
    One thing, the young man's one hunger, his greatest need
To play with, play for love; he will so far succeed
    That she will come and stay two nights, quite properly
'On Mrs Neave's side of the house'.

                        But in a week
    He writes in mock disdain of two Oliviers
'How good one is—we, I mean, are!' and jeers in rhyme
    At Virginia and James who 'have been Talking':

'Awful. *How will it end?* they gibber night and day,
 The Quite Advanced. They impudently ache for us.
Will Ka and Rupert marry? Let us pray . . .'

          He sees
 River and meadowsweet and chestnut-trees, the house
Muffled in clematis, the following summer,
 But sitting at a café table in Berlin:

And by that time could tell 'all the secrets of Hell'
 Seriously, that he had dangled laughingly
As bait to fetch the hesitating Ka when he
 Had been drawn to her; and he had learnt them through her.

V

To begin with he was undoubtedly in love
    And she was not—as then (it reads like a bad play)
She was and he was not.
                 A terror suddenly
    At Lulworth that December, and his near collapse;
Her panic and promise and their waiting to meet;
    Verona, Munich, Starnberg . . .

                          Some things we cannot know
And could not show, and some actors need not be called,
    Like Lytton Strachey and Ka's ambidextrous painter.

What had gripped him we know, for all his irony—
    His hunger and thirst for a proud thoroughgoing
And solemn-joyful passion; while one can guess that Ka
    Could never do with less than two men whom she might
Half choose and half refuse, to keep her hesitant
    And happy to be pressed and safely insecure.

It was indeed a breath, a glimpse of that in her
    Which had unloosed in him a hell of jealousy:
The old dread of rejection, of being 'second best',
    Of half-meaning or none; but with a worse, new fear,
That she was too kind and blind, too unsuspecting,
    A child in danger.

                But the same things, dim to both,
That so brought desperation and his plea to her
    Would bring misery to both in full experience.

For how should he forgive, when he had found the wrong—
    Even acknowledging that he himself did wrong,
As half in love with Noel?—that he was rescued

And soothed and strengthened by her body like a strong
Warm hand she gave for comfort (that she had thought would cost
    So little, for so much); but that he then would find
His full gratitude and tenderness and trust befooled,
    Scorched and smirched by the truth of her as wavering,
Vague, self-deceiving and deceived with the excuse
    That 'There's no need for love'.

                    Yet now it was that Ka
Would in her turn, too late, give way, answer his pain
    With pain, and cling. And he was sorry for her too,
Her complete inability to want or be
    One thing, and all her life blurred and bewildered by
What he had made his hope—above all 'honesty',
    And honesty precisely toward love and desire.

But he felt poisoned, suffocated, cauterised
    And terrified to think he might be tied, and tied
Through being her opposite . . .

                  —But to have done with it,
    Rather than run it through, every sore point, and peer
Like those who hovered at them out of Brunswick Square,
    James, Virginia and Lytton: say, they hurried back,
Went to and fro, and 'tugged and jerked', would 'try again
    In May', and so they came again to Germany.
But he is dead, dead, dead, and in the end will say,
    Has courage and will tell her.

                 So in high summer
They met near Bibury, and talked while Justin waited
    On the road in his Opel by the drowsy wood
And yellow wheatfield.
              And we must wait outside too,
    Until they come back to the car, the broken thing
Between them, and in silence they all drive away.

VI

Two and a half years later the interpreter
　Wrote in Greek with a pencil on the wooden cross
In Skyros
　　　SERVANT OF GOD AND SUB-LIEUTENANT
IN THE ENGLISH NAVY.
　　　　　　　　　　　Although the case is altered
From anything the man knew, or most others then,
　The bare foreign words are like a lucky throw of dice,
Whatever meanings we withhold or attribute
　To God, and may have faded or live on in England.

We cannot in reason think others will agree,
　And but feel our way in half-light. But we follow him
In taking the pit and trap of that experience
　As a kind of death, a death-bed.

　　　　　　　　　　Thus Der Guotaerë,
A gaunt-minded Old German poet, has a knight
　Who lies in danger of death and sees a lady
Come to his bedside, dressed in gold and beautiful.
　And she asks him with a smile 'How do you like me?
You have served me all your life. My name is This-World.
　Now I bring you your reward. Look!'
　　　　　　　　　　　　And she turns her back,
And he sees it is dark, fleshless, a hollow thing
　Crawling with worms and beetles, and stinks like a dead dog.

'Alas, why did I ever serve you?' the knight cries.

Will that seem too antique and grim for such a modern,
One who even in the misery that came with Ka,
　Half-choking in darkness and profounder terror

Could wonder which of them had been the greater fool?

And outwardly there were the two more years of youth
Ranging and shining out more widely.
                                        But the truth is
    That was the way and sign of a new light in darkness.

For even if he had trapped himself, or rather
    Because his deepest self like an avenging angel
Had rounded on him sword in hand, confronting him
    With a joy in defiance: he had seen at last
That the division between what he seemed and dreamed
    To have and be, and the dunghill reality,
Was life, hope, and the truth that he must live and be;
    And everything stood still but meant another thing.

So the war, he admitted (he could never not see)
    Might look like a way out.

                            But after sixty years
I find it the more moving that there was to be
    No visible defeat, but death and victory.
How else, when the decision of that other war
    Of self-betrayal and truth, in unfulfilment,
Without the plain rich payment down of a young death
    Might seem too hard, narrowly like no victory
At all?

    And we cannot doubt that he would rather
    Be dead, with the completed story incomplete,
Than live to grow old, eat dirt and be satisfied.

A Last Attachment

A Last Attachment

1

Spenser has Britomart on guard in the enchanter's house
    Reading over every iron door 'Be bold',
And on and on 'Be bold', until over the last door
    'Be not too bold.'
                    One might vary it: 'Be plain,
Be sad, true, deep'—see with the addition how they do.
    But for the bundle we have here (including
Not only the diary and letters found in a loft
    Among lumber and waste paper by a boy
Who played and rummaged) the only right word is 'Be late.'

    Which is, even with 'Be not too late', I daresay
No famous old device, but vows to serve Eliza
    And Yorick and the *Journal to Eliza*;

2

And will fit it down to the opening, out of things unknown
    And just as he left it, the first pages gone,
Sent after her; when Sterne, worn by so many fevers
    But most that of his heart, sits with her picture
Alone, pale and bereft, in Bond Street:
                       'O my Bramine,
    my friend, my helpmate!'
                      The *Lord Chatham* her ship,
East Indiaman waiting in the Downs, the first fair wind
    Proceeding, had now borne off, stood off with her
And his letters of two weeks, farewells each tenderer
    And wilder than the last, and the last telling
How 'the blood broke from his heart' and 'this poor fine-spun frame
    gave way . . . I fell asleep at last through weakness,

and dreamt thou camest into the Room where I was sitting,
    carrying a shawl. My spirit had flown to thee
with tidings of my fate—you came to bid me comfort,
    folded the shawl about my Waist and kneeling
supplicated my blessing . . .
                       I awoke but Oh my God,
    how broken, sobbing—the bosom of my shirt
brine-wet, steep'd in my tears!'

      3
                  'A month has pass'd, in two months
    you will have doubled the Cape—I'll trace thy track.'
So he scrawls, quivering: 'loose touches of an honest heart'
    'projecting happiness' 'the Ache of doubt—doubt,
did I say? but have none; cross it out . . .'
                      Poor fool, poor wit,
    So caught by *La Belle Indian*, the unhappy

Eliza Draper—young, 'handsome genteel engaging',
    But unhappy above all. What else had given her
'that bewitching sort of nameless excellence'—had left
    'a something in the voice and eyes' traced faintly
By obscure misgiving pains, feeling herself unloved
    By the hard husband in Bombay—who pays for all,
And now recalls her?
                But *now*—'I will live on for thee and for
    my Lydia—gain Fame, gain wisdom in old age,
be rich for the dear children of my heart—to share it all.'

And 'surely—surely thou art mine, Eliza,
for I have bought thee dear! Remember what I suffer—
Pale Ghost! Yea, from the Tables of thy memory . . .

4

'But no, I'll live for thee, live on—count me immortal,
   and do thou press for the ends we have propos'd.'

They were, first, that Draper be convinced that for her health
   She must come back to England, to friends, children
And Yorick—Yorick would meet her on the shore and then—
   Then!
         'I am fitting up a sweet Apartment
here at Coxwold in my thatch'd palace—a neat simple
   Room overlook'd only by the sun; four chairs,
table and Sopha, book-case and bureau—to be all yours:
   I shall see thee the goddess of this temple . . .'

And 'now you are stretching out over in the Trade winds,
   you will arrive at Bombay in October,

by February I shall surely hear—and that you come
   in person, by September.'
              He is persuaded
She would feel 'a monitory sympathetic Shock',
   Were his life threatened; thinks nobody on earth
So like him, his turn of mind, and *knows* she is writing
   At that moment as he writes:
              'My Wife elect,
child of my heart! blessèd and dear to all who know you—
   to me most, only because *I know you best*;
by that love-philtre thou hast charm'd me and wilt ever,
   distance and Time and change can never change this.'

5

And for the *Journey* he 'has her picture off by heart';
   O Cupid, prince of God and men—the fragment

Chants it, her absent presence; he points it with her name,
   'the pure flame of Eliza.' To have and have not
Throbs in remembered France, and Abdera as in Yorkshire:
   'O delicious country air, at peace with all things—
one day I hope you'll like it . . .'
                          'I hope and hope each week,
   each day and hour of it—hunger for some word,
tidings of comfort; we taste not of it now but will—
   full Meals, hereafter!'

              And if he prophesied
A commentator on 'the lady Yorick speaks of'
   ('Her name was Draper') he would smile, not wonder
If he could see his own Smelfungus and Mundungus
   As they lay hands on this reliquary; peer,

Prod and finger it and sniff, compress their lips and cry:
   'He wrote to practise sentiment' 'Cheat, *poseur*'
'Tells downright lies of being ill'
                       'Fibs to her about dates,
   his wife's arrival—to break it off'
                           'Not Sterne
but Yorick plays the fool, sighs, laughs and cries and even
   bleeds and dies, but it is art and effigy . . .'

Or else more kindly: 'Well, he was ill, he lost control,
   but sobered. It must have come to seem unreal.'

6

Unreal. *There* is a thought, there you did well, Mundungus!
    So much for the lost haunted and sick-hearted,
Sick-thoughted Yorick; tired of dining out and yearning
    For 'Cox' and books and solitude—'retiring

to my Room to tell my dear this—count the hours of joy
    pass'd with her, and Meditate those in reserve.
Dear *Enthusiasm!* that brings things forward in a trice
    Time keeps for ages back . . .'

                                        Not a year later
He died, but in another solitude than Coxwold.
    'A very great favourite of the gentlemen's,
who were all very sorry and much lamented him',
    Said Crawfurd's footman who was sent to inquire
From a full-flowing dinner of dukes, earls and nabobs
    To those good lodgings over the silk-bag shop
In Bond Street, and saw him die.
                                        'Now it is come' said Sterne,
    And put up his hand as if to stop a blow.

And was buried in Bayswater, not the hollow shell
    Of Byland Abbey nearby Cordelia's tomb,
Where he would sit 'quite Alone, deep in that sweet recess
    which brightens at the thought of you, and you *here*.
Delusive moments! . . .'

According to La Rochefoucauld
A man in his old age becomes both wiser
And more foolish—*fou et sage.*

And Sterne at fifty-three
(But he says 'ninety-five in constitution')
Might see it, as he showed her picture, ran through her virtues,
Sorrows and charms—half see it as his auditors
Did, as a folly of the King of Denmark's jester;
And yet be wed to it as final wisdom.

And granting the foolishness, we also must see more,
And take it all, sad tender and laughing; take
Those too pointed details of his illness used to amuse,
Confide and disavow; take that too easy tone
For the unwelcome 'restless unreasonable Wife'
Who must be sped back to France. (And why may she
And Draper then in a joint rapid demise, not free
Their loving selves?)

For his pen running after
These and less impudent vanities—like Scarborough,
York Races, dining well with the Archbishop,
And the public prints that rumour him among the wits
At Crazy Hall—turns all to grace and flattery:

'This is a year of presents: from Lord Spencer a grand
new Ecritoire—from Paris a gold snuff-box;
but a portrait worth them both. Sculptures from Ovid's tomb . . .
Oh and last of all a Heart—so finely set!
If I keep it I'll be rich—but lose it, poor indeed.
I must come begging at your Gates . . .'

8

'Poor Yorick!'
But why poor, to end in wit, love, music? Why but because
   The ending was to so much that had ended?

'Jesus, grant me but this' he cries 'I will deserve it',
   Of a young woman, a young half-injured life
He will bid for as a last best pearl, 'that friendly balm
   All-heal of my past evils'; and there in her,

Strangely we see concentred, living, that 'Be late—Be
   not too late' of his brief headlong art and fame.
Both came when youth had gone with all its nonsense, tooling
   And fooling and even the one perfect thing
(If he had that) yet leaving hope, dream, desire alive
   But caught fast.
             'I can't get out' the starling said.

And his gambol of wit, from star-crazed innuendo
   To the blank or marbled page, was born of that:
Would try, cry for a way out, fling, tumble out a way,
   Dance, babble it, tease, pray.
                But there is no way,
Then or now, none. The way is only what he has done
   And does, counting it 'one, a singular blessing

of his life to have been almost every hour of it
   miserably in love.'
          And so how can—how
Can it be too late?

9

'Time goes on slowly, hours like days,
days like weeks—years! while distance grows between us.
But soon it will be shortening, I shall be on the rack—
Come—come! . . .'
                        The loving fool hopes on in prison,
Lives and dies, dying, living and bidding on—for what?
'The Lady for whose company he languish'd'?

Well, that of course. Yet he says 'Our passions ebb and flow.
The truth is thou hast but turn'd them all one way—
they flow to thee.' And there, there is the lucidity
That seeks an old delight, but new in sadness—

Late and yet late, the better.
                        And what if prophecy
And tongues of old gods witness with the *Journal*
And the *Journey* and Spenser's fair-haired girl in armour
To the paradise in sadness, and that one
Smiling mock-true blessing he clung to?
                        Nothing in the end
Could have been easier for Sterne than others.

What we dread for ourselves may be more real to us.
But we see he had to bid, buy with his heart's blood
A hope that looks either a little mad or quite mad;
And then to burn out that 'weak taper of life'
With added flame, and through a body like old paper
That tears easily—to look, love and work on.

Notes

65 *Apollo and the Sibyl*

The Sibyl of Cumae was loved in her youth by Apollo, who offered to grant any wish she might express. She asked to live as many years as there were grains in a certain heap of dust, but forgot to ask for enduring youth. This too would have been granted her, if she had accepted Apollo's love. Refusing it, she lived on to become a prophetess, and at last only a voice, haunting her cave at Cumae.

86 *Cœur de Lion*

On his way back from Syria, Richard Cœur de Lion was taken prisoner by Leopold of Austria, and held to ransom for nearly two years. This poem is suggested by a song, 'Ja nus hom pris', which he composed in captivity.

89 *Les Congés du Lépreux*

The title and theme come from *Les Congiés*, a poem of several hundred lines by Jean Bodel, a poet of Arras in the early thirteenth century. Having become a leper, he took farewell of his friends in these verses; a selection and translation are given by André Mary in *La Fleur de la Poésie Française*, Paris, 1951.

94 *Strambotti*

Strambotti have not been written in English since Sir Thomas Wyatt introduced them from Italy. He translated several from Serafino dell' Aquila, and also used the form for some epigrams referring to his own career. *Strambotti* became fashionable in Italy in the fifteenth century, after a Venetian nobleman, Leonardo Giustinian, had used them to combine themes from folk-song with a more delicate formal discipline. Giustinian's collection of twenty-seven *strambotti* was printed towards the end of the fifteenth century (see *Leonardo Giustinian*, by Manlio Dazzi, Bari, 1934); but these poems were widely known and sung earlier. Collections of folk-songs made in Italy in the nineteenth century, such as Tigri's *Canti*

Popolari Toscani, show that peasants were still singing *rispetti* and other poems of the kind Giustinian knew.

121   *Memoirs in Oxford*

I have revised the text printed in 1970, lightly in some places, heavily in others. My use of the five-line stanza was suggested by Shelley's *Peter Bell the Third*.

The 'imperfect saint' of Section III is Angela of Foligno, who died in 1308. My information comes from a study by Louis Leclève.

149   *Drypoints of the Hasidim*

The limits of my knowledge and understanding of Hasidism will be obvious. If the poem finds any Jewish readers I hope they will be indulgent, and bear in mind that I have had to approach the subject from within a different religious tradition.

My information has come chiefly from the following books:

Martin Buber, *Tales of the Hasidim* The Early Masters
(London, 1956)
Tales of the Hasidim The Later Masters
(New York, 1948)
Louis I. Newman, *The Hasidic Anthology* (New York, 1944)
Gershom G. Scholem, *Major Trends in Jewish Mysticism*
(London, 1955)
Jean de Menasce, *Quand Israël Aime Dieu* (Paris, 1931)
Louis I. Newman, *Maggidim and Hasidim: Their Wisdom*
(New York, 1962)
Louis Jacobs, *Hasidic Prayer* (London, 1972)

In the following notes I have not been able to gloss every reference.

Title: 'Plates are some times engraved in pure dry-point with the bur left ready to catch the printer's ink. This is not really etching. . . . But it is an etcher's process.

'The reader must not think of dry-point as a thin and meagre art. It may be made to look very rich. . . . The hand is not nearly so free as it is in etching, and this objection, together with the serious one that dry-points will not safely yield large

editions, has caused etchers' dry-point to be much neglected.'
(P. G. Hamerton, *Etching and Etchers*, London, 1876, p. 440.)

149   I. 1: I am thinking of names such as Elimelech of Lizhensk (d. 1786), Aaron of Karlin (d. 1772), etc.

150   I. 2: *yeshivahs*: local institutions for Talmudic studies.

151   I. 3: Dov Baer: a disciple of the Baal Shem, d. 1772.
Maggid: preacher.

152   I. 4: Shekhinah: 'divine hypostasis indwelling in the world and sharing the exile of Israel; Divine Presence among men' ('The Later Masters', p. 336).

Other references in this section are to Martin Buber, *The Legend of the Baal-Shem* (London, 1956) and Newman, *The Hasidic Anthology*, p. 57.

153   II. 1: see 'The Early Masters', p. 64.
zaddik: 'the leader of the Hasidic community' (Buber).
the Besht: the Baal Shem Tov (1700–60), the founder of Hasidism; see 'The Early Masters', p. 78, and Scholem, p. 330.

154   II. 2, 3: These sections draw on Scholem's account of Sabbatianism and the origins of Hasidism (pp. 287–334). As Scholem explains in discussing the Zohar and Sabbatianism, the conceptions of the 'holy sparks' and the *kelipoth* are interdependent. The Zohar interprets evil as 'a sort of residue or refuse of the hidden life's organic process' (p. 238); one of the metaphors conveying this doctrine is that of 'evil as the *Kelipah*, or the "bark" of the cosmic tree or the "shell" of the nut' (p. 239). Isaac Luria (1514–72) developed the idea of 'the fall of divine "sparks of light" from the divine realm to the lower depths' (p. 268); there they are imprisoned in the *kelipoth* or 'shells', from which they have to be liberated by human effort, if 'the ideal order' of creation is to be restored.

155   II. 3: Sabbatai Zevi: 1625–76. He proclaimed himself Messiah and drew many followers; but apostatised to Islam after being imprisoned by the Ottomans. According to Scholem, 'he was the living archetype of the paradox of the holy sinner' (see pp. 289–94).
Torah: 'teaching, law, both the written (biblical) and the oral (traditional) law' (Buber).

156   II. 4: *kawannoth*: plural of *kawannah*, 'the intention directed towards God while performing a (religious) deed' (Buber). See Scholem, p. 275; and Jacobs, chapters III and VI.

156   Bunam: Simha Bunam of Parsischa, d. 1827. See 'The Later Masters', p. 240.

157   III. 1: Messiah son of Joseph: 'a Messiah who will prepare the way. ... Another tradition holds that he reappears "from generation to generation"' (Buber). See 'The Later Masters', p. 151.

158   III. 3: Jacob Joseph of Polnoye: d. about 1775; a disciple of the Besht.
    Yisakhar Baer: d. 1843.

159   III. 4: Zevi Hirsh: of Zhydatchov; d. 1831. For the reference to Isaac, see *Genesis*, 24.63.

160   III. 5: the Yehudi: 'the Jew'; Yaakov Yitzhak of Parsischa, d. 1814. Kalman of Cracow: d. 1823. He was a disciple of Elimelech of Lizhensk and 'the Seer' of Lublin (see below, IV. 4).
    Shelomo Leib: of Lentshno; d. 1843.
    III. 6: the Rabbi of Berditchev: d. 1809. The story really belongs to the Rabbi of Apt, Abraham Yehoshua Heshel (d. 1822); see 'The Later Masters', p. 120.

161   III. 7: Hayyim of Zans: d. 1876.

162   IV. 1: *mitnaggedim*: 'the avowed opponents of Hasidism' (Buber). 'Germans': see 'The Later Masters', p. 240.
    Poles: see 'The Early Masters', p. 188.

163   IV. 2: 'It is so': see Buber, *The Legend of the Baal-Shem*, p. 174. 'I have a secret': see Dobh Baer of Lubavitch, *Tract on Ecstasy*, translated by Louis Jacobs (London, 1968), pp. 57, 175. The author was a godson of Dov Baer of Mesritch (see I. 3). The *Tract* is a theory and vindication of ecstatic prayer.

164   IV. 4: Menahem Mendel: of Kotzk; d. 1859. See 'The Later Masters', pp. 39–43 and 270–89; and Scholem, p. 345.
    the Rabbi of Lublin: Yaakov Yitzhak, 'the Seer'; d. 1815. See 'The Early Masters', pp. 300–18.

166   IV. 5: Schneor Zalman: of Ladi; d. 1813. He was 'the Rav' of Northern White Russia. See 'The Early Masters', pp. 265–72.

168   V. 2: the son of Jesse: See Newman, *The Hasidic Anthology*, pp. 247–8.
    Israel of Rizhyn: d. 1850. See 'The Later Masters', pp. 15–16; and Scholem, p. 337.

171   *Afterword on Rupert Brooke*

The main sources are Christopher Hassall's biography (1964) and Sir Geoffrey Keynes's edition of the *Letters* (1968).

The verse is syllabic, in the measure of twelve syllables devised by Robert Bridges. His best-known poem in this metre is *The Testament of Beauty* (1930). But *Poor Poll* (1921) was his first illustration of its potentialities, and is the best guide to its structure. I have allowed myself fewer 'elisions' than one finds in *The Testament of Beauty*, and aimed at a greater variety of rhythm.

187   *A Last Attachment*

The manuscript of Sterne's *Journal to Eliza* was discovered in the nineteenth century and first printed in 1904. It was written between April and August, 1767. In June of that year Sterne set to work on the *Sentimental Journey*, which appeared in February 1768, a month before his death.

Eliza was 22 when Sterne met her in the winter of 1766. At the age of 14 she had been married to Daniel Draper, an official of the East India Company in Bombay. She had two children by him, who came to England with her in 1765 and were left there at school when she returned to India in 1767. She eventually left her husband and came to England, where she died in 1778.

Index of Titles and First Lines

(first lines are in *italic*, subtitles in SMALL CAPITALS)

Date Due
